Realistic Model Railroad
BUILDING BLOCKS

An introduction to Layout Design Elements

Tony Koester

KALMBACH
BOOKS

Acknowledgments

I credited those who have contributed photos and other key bits of information for this book in the captions or text, but several friends and commercial suppliers have gone out of their way to help. Among them are Bob's Photos, Don Daily, Mallory Hope Ferrell, Chuck Hitchcock, Steve King, Bill Miller, John Nehrich, Perry Squier, Tony Steele, John Swanson, Joe Weaver, and Stan White. Last but not least, working with Lawrence Hansen of Kalmbach Books was a pleasure.

—Tony Koester
Newton, N.J.
April 2005

Printed in the United States of America

05 06 07 08 09 10 11 12 13 14   10 9 8 7 6 5 4 3 2 1

Visit our website at http://kalmbachbooks.com
Secure online ordering available.
Questions or comments? E-mail us at books@kalmbach.com

Publisher's Cataloging-In-Publication Data
(Prepared by The Donohue Group, Inc.)

Koester, Tony.
    Realistic model railroad building blocks : an introduction to layout design elements/ Tony Koester.

    p. : ill. ; cm.
    ISBN: 0-89024-368-9

1.   Railroads—Models—Design and construction—Handbooks, manuals, etc.   I. Title.

TF197 .K64 2005
625.19

Senior editor: Lawrence Hansen
Editorial associate: Lesley Weiss
Managing art director: Michael Soliday
Art director/book design: Tom Ford
Photos and illustrations: Tony Koester (unless otherwise noted)

Some track plans in this book were previously published in past issues of *Model Railroader* and *Model Railroad Planning*.

Contents

Matt Kosic

Introduction

Long before the author introduced the term "Layout Design Element," Arnt Gerritsen used this approach to faithfully model the Ann Arbor RR in HO, including this waterfront scene at Frankfort, Mich. (see Chapter 9).

Perhaps the most fundamental and challenging step in building a model railroad is track planning. Like building a poor foundation, doing a poor job at that early juncture almost ensures that the results won't live up to our expectations. But since track planning occurs so early in the process, it often must be done when we're still on the steep part of the learning curve. At that point, the basic requirements of a good plan, one that will offer both building and operating enjoyment in the months and years ahead, aren't as well defined as they should be. Wouldn't it be nice if we had some magic formula to help us create plausible plans for our railroads now rather than later?

Actually, we do: Layout Design Elements. LDEs are visually and operationally recognizable models of specific prototype towns, junctions, industries, yards, engine terminals, scenes, bridges, and ports.

I introduced this building-block concept in the inaugural (1995) issue of *Model Railroad Planning*. Think of it as a connect-the-dots or jigsaw-puzzle approach to layout design. The premise is simple: Look to the full-size ("prototype") railroads for guidance when designing a model railroad, be it freelanced (not based on a specific "real" railroad) or prototype-based. If each building block (LDE) is simply a copy of key elements of a specific prototypical track arrangement, we can be reasonably sure that our model railroad will look realistic and operate plausibly. Stringing several LDEs together completes the picture.

The alternative is to reinvent the wheel: Start with a clean sheet of paper or a blank computer screen and arrange tracks and turnouts and crossings in what we hope will be a visually pleasing and operationally interesting configuration. To do this well, we need a solid schooling in the fundamentals of prototype railroading. While we'll probably acquire that knowledge over the years, we may not have it in abundance at the time we start planning our layouts.

All it takes is a caboose track (you did include a caboose track, didn't you?) on the wrong side of the main line in a yard, an engine lead that trips up yard crews every time a locomotive heads for or leaves the engine terminal, or the lack of a crossover at a key location to make a railroad far more difficult—and less enjoyable—to operate than it should be. Even if we profess not to be interested in realistic operation, odds are that we still want to run our trains in a manner complementing their realistic appearance.

That's where Layout Design Elements come in. Each one represents a well-considered step toward a model railroad that will be as much fun to operate as it is to build and scenic. Several of them plausibly strung together almost ensure that

the resulting model railroad will offer realism and operational rewards beyond anything we might make up.

Those who model a specific prototype, as I now do, tend to employ LDEs by default. We choose a favorite full-size railroad, then refine that goal by selecting a manageable, model-worthy segment of it—a major terminal or part of a division or subdivision. Finally, we further distill that choice by picking key towns and scenes along the line.

The freelancer may seem to be out of luck. The usual reasons given for freelancing are a lack of knowledge of or interest in a specific prototype (how can you model what you don't understand?), or a desire to model facets of full-size railroading that no single prototype encompasses.

But freelancers can use the LDE building-block approach by choosing a prototype or prototypes in a given region and era. If you want to model an Appalachian coal hauler, for example, you would want to study the Western Maryland, Virginian, Clinchfield, Norfolk & Western, Baltimore & Ohio, Chesapeake & Ohio, or Southern of the 1950s or '60s or CSX or Norfolk Southern today.

The real advantage comes as you move from the design phase to the construction phase. In all likelihood, you won't know much about several of the LDEs you have selected. Since you based the freelanced track plan and structures on a specific prototype or two, however, you can press forward knowing that everything will work out just fine in the end. After all, it did for the full-sized railroad!

Now that you've gained some insight into the purpose of LDEs, we'll first take a look at choosing them and where to obtain the needed information. Then we'll identify specific LDE candidates of each basic type, examine several in detail, and look at some options. Finally, we'll convert LDEs to "puzzle pieces" and connect them together to form two new track plans.

This process paid major dividends for me as my current model railroad took shape. I hope it proves equally helpful to you.

John W. Maxwell

CHAPTER ONE

Layout Design Elements

▲ A popular prototype for narrow-gauge modelers is the former Colorado & Southern. Here, low-slung C&S no. 70 is switching the Argo Tunnel Mine at Idaho Springs, Colo. Part of the line at Clear Creek Canyon has been restored for tourist train operation, and much of the abandoned portion of the line is still visible.

As an editor of a model railroad magazine for much of my career, and as a communicator of technical concepts for all of it, I have always sought ways to make challenging concepts easier to grasp and difficult chores easier to accomplish. One way to do this is to reduce everything to some sort of formula or matrix—a standardized approach that will get you to your goal most of the time. (There is no "universal solvent.")

LDEs for freelancing?

That led me to the Layout Design Element (LDE) approach to track planning. The concept may seem obvious in the context of prototype modeling, although some "prototype" layouts do come up short in this regard—too much inspiration (reinventing the wheel) and not enough perspiration (doing some homework), perhaps. But the more I thought about it, the clearer it became that using prototype-based building blocks applies equally to freelancing (figs. 1-1 and 1-2).

Prototype modelers often have a tremendous advantage over freelancers in that there are benchmarks—the prototype—for everything. What color should depots be painted? Look to the prototype's example. How should the trackage in Danville be arranged? Check the prototype. What did the railroad deliver to that warehouse? Ask someone who worked there. Why was there a crossover west of 10th St.? Include it and hope its purpose becomes clear as you try to switch the local industries, or ask a professional who worked that line what it was for.

The key question was whether this approach could also help the freelancer, especially someone who at this juncture doesn't know much about how railroads went about making a living, yet finds model trains fascinating. Those are the folks who really need support and guidance. I'm happy to report that in the decade that has passed since I introduced the LDE concept in *Model Railroad Planning*, I've found that the answer is an emphatic "Yes!"

Helping without stifling

Many modelers freelance because they simply don't know much about any specific prototype, or at least not enough to make modeling it faithfully seem enjoyable. Others are true free spirits who don't want to be bound by rules and regulations. They may not even be railfans but are rather simply enamored by miniature trains and the trappings that surround them.

The problem is that, to quote Jim Boyd, former editor of *Railfan* and *Railroad* magazines, there is a

▲ Harry Brunk's HOn3 Union Central & Northern is freelanced but is accurately based on the Colorado & Southern's line at Clear Creek Canyon, as this model photo of the Argo Tunnel mine (see fig. 1-1) clearly shows. His entire layout is a series of Layout Design Elements strung end to end, as shown in his track plan in the 2002 issue of *Model Railroad Planning*.

universality to railroading. Large or small, railroads are bound by many of the same physical constraints. If you want to pick up a car from a facing-point spur (where the locomotive encounters the switchpoints before the frog), to get that car behind the engine requires a runaround move, hence a runaround track. To switch a "dog's breakfast" (Jim again) of freight cars in an arriving local into blocks of cars and then into trains headed for specific distant destinations, you need only two yard tracks (more are handy but not required) to make put-and-take moves.

This applies to a model railroad just as much as to a full-size enterprise. Those who operate their railroads

realistically have either discovered these and other "rules" through trial and error or have learned from the experiences of others.

Trends

There are several obvious trends in the hobby. Sound effects, both on and off our trains, are coming into greater use, as is command control. Prototype modeling is more popular than ever (fig. 1-3, page 8), as is the use of couplers and wheels that are closer to scale. And although surveys indicate that less than a fifth of those who read the scale model railroad magazines consider themselves "operators," the popularity of realistic operation has certainly grown remarkably in the last

Top: Modeling a specific prototype at a specific location is an increasingly popular approach to layout planning. This is Jeff Wilson's HO model of the junction in Portage, Illinois, where the Illinois Central and the Chicago, Burlington & Quincy cross, ca. 1964. To make things even more interesting, a Chicago Great Western freight rolls through the junction (CGW had trackage rights to use CB&Q track). Bottom: Mike Nelson photographed CGW train 91 headed westbound through the actual scene on March 9, 1966.

1-3

quarter century. My book *Realistic Model Railroad Operation* was into its second printing within two years of its debut in 2003.

What this suggests is that many of those who now profess no interest in operation will grow into it. That, in turn, tells me that it would pay for anyone, and everyone, to use prototypical trackwork designs when building his or her next model railroad. That way, should the operating bug bite, the railroad will be ready and waiting for the opportunity to strut its stuff.

Ah, but there's a catch: The very folks who should plan ahead for such an eventuality are the same folks who haven't a clue as to how to design and build prototypically plausible trackwork. And the rest of us probably aren't quite as good at it as we assume.

What are we to do?

Prototype plagiarism

The point of this book is plagiarism: Copy the prototype—within reason, of course. Few of us have enough space to model even one town foot-for-foot in our train room, which became crystal clear to Mike Aufderheide when he overlaid an HO plan of Monon, Ind., on a same-scale drawing of his basement (fig. 1-4). It consumed the entire area! Selective compression was obviously required so that Mike could also model several other towns along the Hoosier Line.

Even if we had gymnasium-size basements and could copy our favorite prototypes inch for inch, where would we ever find the resources—time, energy, and money—to populate them with model railroads of that size and scope? The LDE approach to layout design therefore has to be tempered with judicious selective compression—reproducing some of the prototype's elements, not all of them. By choosing towns and other LDE candidates with care and modeling only their key aesthetic and operational features, we can create a practical series of Layout Design Elements and hence plausible model railroads.

Taking the first steps

Let's say that you don't have a space for a complete model railroad right now. You're a student who lives in a dorm, or you're on the road and living out of your suitcase in an endless series of look-alike motel rooms. Odds are that you have a bookcase, so let's focus on the real estate you do have: its top shelf. Why not clean off the stacks of books and put a modest length of insulating foam there instead? You can glue some track on top of that foam to create part of a future model railroad.

Presto! We've transformed the self-defeating, no-space-for-a-layout argument into a debate about what trackage arrangement you could put on that slab of foam or, better yet, one of David Barrow's 18" x 48" plywood-capped dominoes (we'll come back to them later). I, for one, vote for a Layout Design Element.

If you haven't done so before, this is a good time to reflect on the full-size railroad or type of railroad that most interests you. This is the hardest part of all, as the choices are so vast. Just take your best shot for the purposes of this exercise. Besides, there's nothing you can build that you can't unbuild or modify later if your tastes change. That's another advantage of domino construction.

Your library may already contain

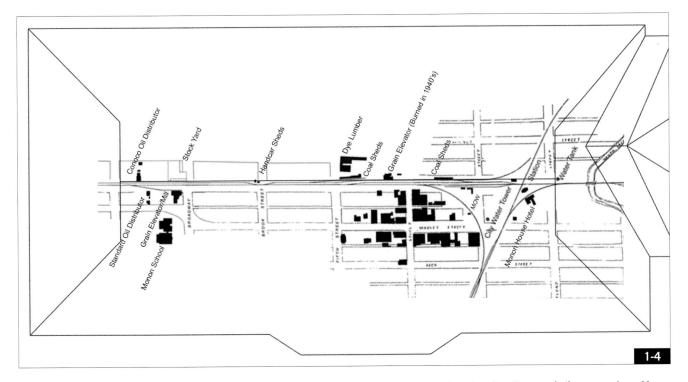

1-4

▲ Modeler Mike Aufderheide discovered that an exact-scale HO model of the Hoosier town of Monon, where the railroad's two main lines crossed, would consume his entire basement! Selective compression resulted in a more manageable LDE depicting the crossing (see *Model Railroad Planning, 2006*).

enough information to get you started. A book or two on your favorite prototype(s) may illustrate any number of potential candidates for Layout Design Elements. If not, the ads in model railroad and railfan magazines will guide you to additional books, magazines, video tapes, CDs, and DVDs brimming over with LDE candidates. Maybe an example in the following chapters will catch your eye. Just try to identify one good LDE candidate; it will lead you to others.

You'll want to join the historical society that is focused on your favorite railroad. Their publication alone may be worth the dues, but even more important are the contacts with other modelers who share your interests and, especially, with professional railroaders who worked on that railroad. As modelers, we have a tendency to interpret what happened at a given time and place without fully understanding the rules of the game; the pros lived it and will quickly set us straight on how it was, and why.

For example, a contract agreement may have required that road crews be paid a higher rate if they had to stop at more than two towns to make even one setout or pickup. If you choose as LDE candidates those towns where through freights often stopped to work because of, say, "hot" cars from an auto-parts plant or a busy interchange with a foreign railroad, you'll have more work for your future crews to do without ignoring normal prototype practices.

If you take but one lesson from this book, this is it: Whether you're a prototype modeler or a freelancer, look to the prototype for inspiration and examples. Talk to the professional railroaders who worked that line to learn how it was really done.

Play now, pay later

LDEs offer two major advantages over the conventional approach to layout design: They help ensure that what you build will look and operate like the prototype, and they let you get started now, long before you acquire a lot of knowledge about why the trackage was arranged as it was or how it was used. You know it worked for the big guys, so it should work just fine for you.

You're not entirely off the hook, however. You usually won't be able to model a complete prototype town or yard inch for inch, although converting

to a smaller scale such as N may help (as Jerry Britton discussed in *Model Railroad Planning* 2005). You'll have to make some considered choices as to what to include and what to leave out. That's called selective compression, and it applies to prototypically based track design as much as to structures.

Fig. 1-5 (page 10) shows how I retained the essentials on my own layout. A rather complex, spread-out series of sidings on either side of the Nickel Plate Road-Peoria & Eastern (later Norfolk & Western-Penn Central) crossing at Veedersburg, Ind., has been reduced to a simpler, more compact configuration. What's important is that the trackwork still mimics the prototype in that the interchange and several spurs and curves are still modeled.

Source of motivation

Instead of being a handicap, your current search for an LDE candidate will motivate you to learn more about how your chosen bit of prototype railroading looked and functioned in the era you've selected. I've found that doing this kind of "homework" is as exciting as trying to solve a great

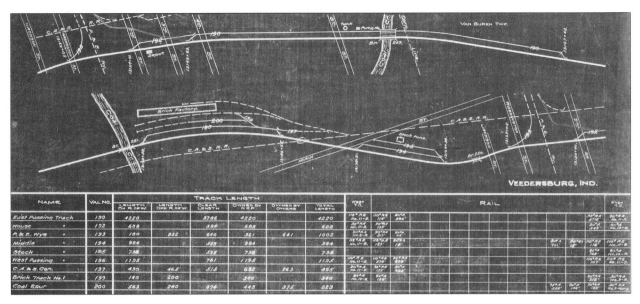

NAME	VAL.NO.	TRACK LENGTH						WEST T.O.	RAIL	EAST T.O.
		LENGTH ON R.OF W.	LENGTH OFF R.OF W.	CLEAR LENGTH	OWNED BY NKP	OWNED BY OTHERS	TOTAL LENGTH			
East Passing Track	190	4220		3766	4220		4220			
House	192	608		388	608		608			
P.&E. Wye	193	180	822	640	361	641	1002			
Middle	194	984		549	984		984			
Stock	195	738		535	738		738			
West Passing	196	1195		761	1195		1195			
C.A.&S.Con.	197	430	465	515	632	263	895			
Brick Track No.1	199	140	200		340		340			
Coal Spur	200	563	260	894	448	375	823			

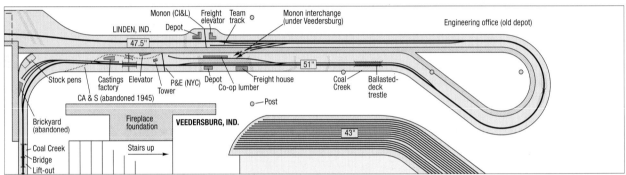

The official Nickel Plate Road track blueprint from the 1940s shows the town of Veedersburg, Ind., where the NKP's St. Louis Division crossed the Peoria & Eastern. The horizontal broken line shows the Chicago, Attica & Southern, which roughly paralleled the NKP through town prior to 1945. The red line was penciled in by a station agent to show post-CA&S-abandonment interchange track changes. Veedersburg was condensed into an LDE for the author's new HO layout.

1-5

mystery before the author lets the cat out of the bag.

Choosing prototype segments to convert to LDEs, and selectively compressing them to fit your available space, is not a foolproof process, as I will discuss in Chapter 2. But it does represent a head start, a logical step forward. For every misstep, you'll probably take many more correct steps. The net result will be positive.

A gallery of options

The following chapters contain examples of towns, junctions, yards, industries, engine terminals, scenes, bridges, and places where rails meet water that can serve as the bases for Layout Design Elements. As you review them, don't lose sight of the main point of using the LDE approach: By looking to the prototype for inspiration and specific track-design information, you have a reasonable degree of assurance that what you design and build will be something plausible, and that it will work as a full-size railroad worked.

By identifying LDE candidates and then doing a modicum of homework to gather information and pinpoint their key attributes, you'll broaden the basis of your hobby from pure model building to industrial archeology. My experience and that of many others strongly suggests that, rather than being a time-consuming obstacle, data gathering will become an adjunct to your leisure-time activities every bit as enjoyable as modeling.

One caveat: You can't possibly learn everything about anything, so don't get into an analysis-paralysis mode. A major advantage of the LDE approach is that, since your modeling is based on actual places on one or more prototype railroads, you can start work confident the resulting LDEs will work for you just as well as they did on the prototypes.

So let's get started by taking a closer look at some towns that can serve as prototypes for LDEs, starting with a key one I selected for my new model railroad.

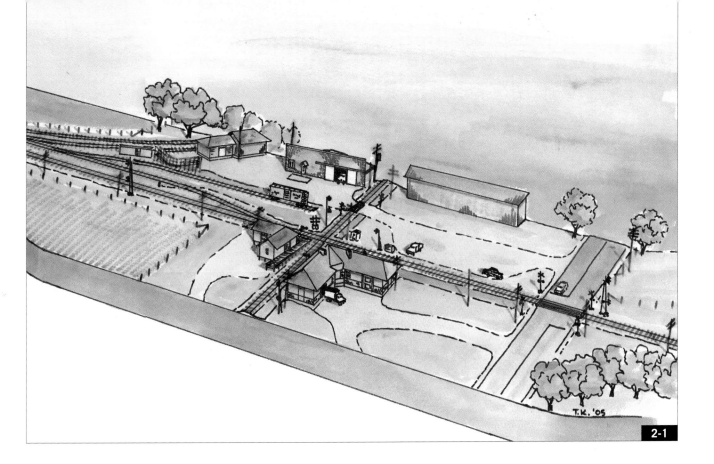

2-1

CHAPTER TWO
Towns and cities

As good an example of a town Layout Design Element as Linden, Ind., is (figs. 2-1 and 2-2), the town nearly didn't make it onto my layout at all. As I was selecting towns for my new HO model railroad a few years ago, Linden didn't even make the cut. There was nothing wrong with Linden; my selection criteria were at fault.

▲ An L-shaped wood depot marked the crossing of the Nickel Plate's St. Louis line with the Monon's main line to Louisville, Ky.

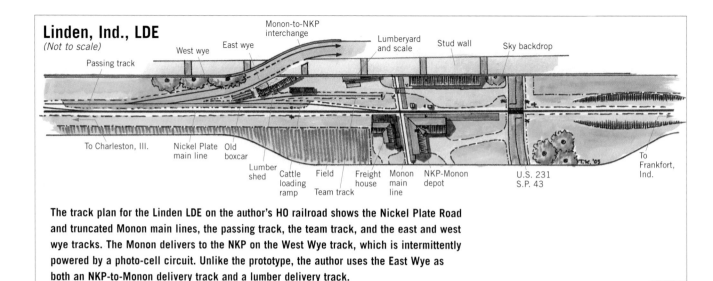

Linden, Ind., LDE
(Not to scale)

Monon-to-NKP interchange

West wye   East wye   Lumberyard and scale   Stud wall   Sky backdrop

Passing track

To Charleston, Ill.   Nickel Plate main line   Old boxcar

Lumber shed   Cattle loading ramp   Field   Freight house   Monon main line   NKP-Monon depot   U.S. 231 S.P. 43   To Frankfort, Ind.

Team track

The track plan for the Linden LDE on the author's HO railroad shows the Nickel Plate Road and truncated Monon main lines, the passing track, the team track, and the east and west wye tracks. The Monon delivers to the NKP on the West Wye track, which is intermittently powered by a photo-cell circuit. Unlike the prototype, the author uses the East Wye as both an NKP-to-Monon delivery track and a lumber delivery track.

2-2

Matching LDEs to goals

The nearby Hoosier town of Wingate was my initial choice for this "slot" on the railroad. That's because, with friends Jon Marx and Bob Walker, I had thoroughly documented Wingate during a field trip way back in 1970. I took lots of photos of the two grain elevators and the NKP's wood depot there, and we even measured the depot.

That information was converted into scale drawings of the depot, which appeared in the March 1995 issue of *Model Railroader*. I also used Wingate to introduce the LDE concept in *Model Railroad Planning* 1995. It seemed silly not to model a town that was so well documented.

But there was a problem. Bill Darnaby, designer and builder of the freelanced HO Maumee Route, pointed out a missed opportunity: Why, he asked, did I choose a town that didn't include a crossing at grade

with another railroad? In so doing, I was giving up an interchange track between the modeled and a crossing "foreign" railroad.

Why make such a big deal out of swapping one type of industry (the two grain elevators located side by side on a stub-ended track) for another (the interchange track)? Here's where one's modeling goals enter the picture. Had I been building a smaller model railroad with but one or two towns, and with scenery and structures rather than operation as the major goal, Wingate might have been a good LDE candidate. The depot and grain elevators would have made excellent kitbashing or scratchbuilding projects.

A primary purpose in modeling the Third Subdivision of the Nickel Plate Road's main line to St. Louis, however, was to focus on a specific type of operation. I wanted to build a single-track railroad that was dispatched

using the arcane but challenging rules of timetable and train-order operation, which were discussed in my book *Realistic Model Railroad Operation*.

To capture the look and feel of a mid-1950s, high-speed, Midwestern railroad, I needed a long mainline run and at least a half-dozen towns with passing tracks where trains could meet and pass. Notice that I cited "look" as well as "feel." I wanted to literally see the railroad that as a youth I had enjoyed watching during its last four years of steam.

To that end, I chose interesting scenic locations as carefully as I chose key operating sites. But, as Bill pointed out, it was possible to have both; there was no need to ignore the "feel," the operating potential of a busy interchange, just to gain the "look"—two more grain elevators.

These photos of Linden, Ind., by former operator Ralph Blacketer show the area around the NKP–Monon diamond, including the team track and cattle chutes. The photos are displayed inside the depot, which is now a museum.

2-3

Lingering look at Linden

As I pointed out in Chapter 1, the process of gathering information about a potential Layout Design Element is often as much fun as building the resulting model. Each fall, several of us—usually Bill Darnaby, Don Daily, Perry Squier, and I—make what we've come to call a "Third Sub Safari" to gather information. I initially, and naively, thought that one or two such trips would suffice, but every outing uncovers new information.

In the case of Linden, there was an obvious place to start: the Linden-Madison Township Historical Society of Linden, which has restored the NKP-Monon depot that stands at the former junction. (CSX still runs north-south through Linden, but the Norfolk & Western abandoned this part of the NKP in 1989.)

In the depot is a good collection of memorabilia, including some very helpful photographs (fig. 2-3) by former operator Ralph Blacketer and others. Having the actual depot to examine was a plus; we discovered that the wings are not arranged at a right angle, as shown in the drawings in the June 1975 issue of *Model Railroader*. Rather, they are aligned parallel to the two railroads, which crossed at an angle of 81 degrees 33 minutes, as is evident in my sketch and plan view of the Linden LDE (fig. 2-2).

This underscores not only the importance of making field trips to gather and check information but also the benefits derived from the efforts of those who work hard to save railroad history. My hat's off to Joe Weaver and the other officials and members of the museum staff in Linden.

At the time of this writing, Linden was a work-in-progress on my new HO layout. The interchange tracks and circuitry that controls the "metered" interchange (more on that shortly) were in place, as was the foliage that helps disguise the wall opening (fig. 2-4). I had also trimmed a Grandt Line warehouse to fit through and against the right side of the backdrop hole as a test before scratchbuilding the lumber sheds that will actually go there and help disguise the hole in the wall.

▲ Progress on the author's Third Subdivision to date shows the same general area as the LDE sketch. Note how the shed and trees (3-D and painted) help to disguise the hole in the backdrop needed to reach the east and west wye track staging extensions behind the stud wall. The unpainted depot was scratchbuilt by Frank Hodina.

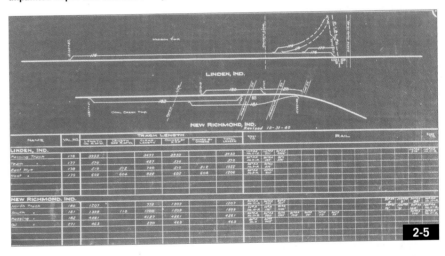

▲ The official NKP track diagram for Linden shows the East and West Wye and Team tracks in the northwest quadrant of the crossing. Not shown is the "short crossover" added just west of the wye turnouts in the late 1940s to make runaround moves easier.

Linden's "industries"

Linden's main attraction as far as operation is concerned is the interchange. According to an official NKP booklet, "Physical Data and Other Information of Interest" for the Clover Leaf Dist. issued in September 1954, the NKP and Monon interchanged approximately 12,000 loaded cars in 1953—4,895 delivered to the Monon, 6,874 received from the Monon. We can assume that a roughly equal number of empties was

routed back to the connecting railroad through the interchange. That's 24,000 cars per year, or about 65 cars daily.

That's some "local industry"! Try to imagine any other small-town industry that could provide so much traffic. Then consider that almost any type of freight car could be exchanged via an interchange—another huge asset. That's why Bill Darnaby had urged me to rethink my choice of LDE candidates.

In the northwest quadrant of the crossing, there was also a team track where cars could be spotted for loading

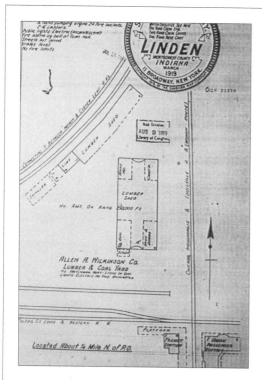

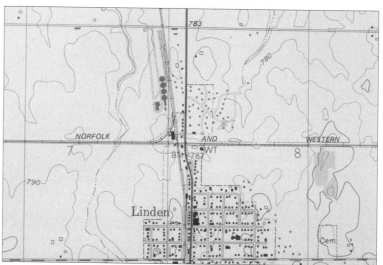

Sanborn fire-insurance and U.S. Geological Survey topographic maps provide considerable information. The Sanborn map of Linden, Ind., dates to 1919 but shows features that were extant in the 1950s. The U.S.G.S. map shows additions since the map was originally drawn in magenta. Among the new features is a grain elevator northwest of the NKP–Monon crossing.

2-6

or unloading by other industries in the area (near the diamond in fig. 2-5, page 13). Alongside the NKP–Monon interchange, officially known as the West Wye track (it looked like one leg of a turning wye, suggesting there may have been a complete wye here at an earlier time), was a track called the East Wye. Cars could be spotted here for unloading into a "shed," actually several buildings. A Sanborn fire-insurance map (fig. 2-6) shows that parts of the shed were used to store lime (used as fertilizer, I assume) and shingles.

Moreover, other drawings and photos showed that livestock could be loaded here. Just beyond the loading chutes was an old boxcar body, perhaps used by the NKP car inspector who checked all interchanged traffic. And down the tracks to the east, just across U.S. Hwy. 231/State Rd. 43, was a wood section house, which I became aware of when perusing old copies of the *Nickel Plate Road Magazine*.

The missing crossover

If an eastbound NKP freight stopped to pick up off the Monon interchange, the locomotive would need to retrieve the car(s) from the interchange by coupling them to its pilot, pulling them off the west wye, then running around them. According to the official NKP track diagram of Linden (fig. 2-5), this would require leaving the train west of town and using the entire length of the passing track to run around.

Sometime in the late 1940s or early 1950s, photos show that a crossover between the main and passing track magically appeared just west of the interchange track. About the same time a crossover near the depot at Veedersburg, Ind. (fig. 1-4), became surplus because of a track reconfiguration (the result of the post-World War II abandonment of the Chicago, Attica & Southern). I suspect it was moved east to Linden.

A lesson for freelancers: The use of such a "short crossover" to avoid long runaround moves is a good design practice.

I had already glued the mainline and passing track flex track down when I discovered the change, making retrofitting the crossover a bit of a pain. But it's not merely cosmetic, so I had little choice. Fortunately, I caught the change in time to avoid installing the crossover that was removed in Veedersburg.

Vertically paired towns

Choosing a suitable town to condense into a Layout Design Element requires thinking in three dimensions if you're building a multi-level layout. For example, Metcalf, Ill., where the Baltimore & Ohio crossed the NKP, is right above Linden on my layout. If crews try to work at both Linden and Metcalf at the same time, won't they get in each other's way?

As I documented on page 77 of *Realistic Model Railroad Design*, this can be avoided by selecting towns where the centers of activity are at opposite ends. At Linden, most work is done near the east end; at Metcalf, the crossing is at the west end of the passing track. Crews therefore tend to be offset from each other as they work.

Other LDE needs

Steam locomotives live on water and fuel (coal or oil). Of the two, water was the one that needed to be replenished more often, perhaps several times during a run over a division. Our choices of LDE candidates for a steam-era railroad must therefore accommodate those needs.

One thing Linden didn't have was a water tank. On the NKP's Third

Subdivision, Berkshires and USRA light Mikados modified with high-capacity tenders could often make a run over a division without stopping for more coal. But it took a lot of skill "hooking up" a steam locomotive and a bit of luck (not being "stabbed" by several foreign-road trains crossing in front of them, for example) to make the run without a water stop.

The daily local freight, however, was seldom so lucky, so I needed to choose at least one town with a water tank as the basis for an LDE. A water tower was located just east of Cayuga, Ind. (fig. 2-7)—my boyhood home town and an obvious LDE candidate for sentimental as well as operational reasons (the NKP crossed the Chicago & Eastern Illinois' hot Chicago–Evansville double-track main line there). Since Cayuga was located near the midpoint of my HO main line, that solved the water problem. (Please refer to the model-vs.-prototype distance graph on page 70 of *Realistic Model Railroad Design*.)

If this sounds academic, consider that Digital Command Control users should soon have the ability to specify the water capacity of each steam locomotive. "Burn" too much water by using excessive throttle or spending too much time switching or "in the hole" waiting for a superior train without stopping for water and the fire has to be dropped—that is, the locomotive ceases to function. It can be reset only at a water tank or coal dock.

A "metered" interchange

An article I prepared for *Model Railroader* describes how I designed a way to let the Monon deliver, say, 30 cars per day (loads and empties) to the NKP at Linden. Moreover, the cars are "metered" to the NKP—not in one long cut but rather in a series of cuts of 6 to 8 cars per cut. Since the Monon main line is only 24" long between the aisle and backdrop, as shown in this chapter's lead illustrations, that required some head-scratching.

This is done by having a Monon diesel on the extended, and hidden, interchange track shove a 30-car cut through a hole in the backdrop into

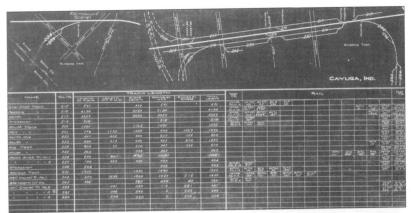

The steel water tower just west of the Wabash River bridge near Cayuga, Ind., is shown on the NKP track diagram and in this evocative portrait by Jesse Lunger of one of the NKP's potent 700-series Berkshires headed west toward Cayuga and Charleston, Ill. 2-7

▲ Stan White built an HO scale LDE depicting the Ma & Pa depot, engine house, and several major industries in York, Pa., in a surprisingly compact area.

▲ The Ma & Pa "roundhouse" at York was actually rectangular. This photo by William Moedinger, Jr., shows gas-electric 62 being turned for a trip back down the line.

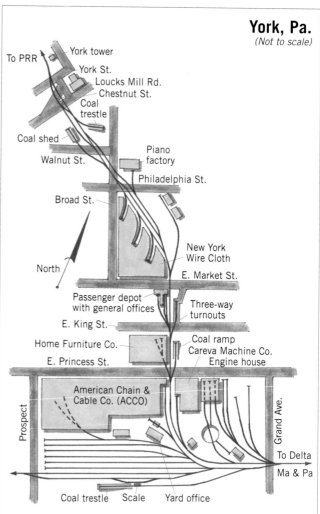

York, Pa.
(Not to scale)

To PRR
York tower
York St.
Loucks Mill Rd.
Chestnut St.
Coal trestle
Coal shed
Walnut St.
Piano factory
Philadelphia St.
Broad St.
North
New York Wire Cloth
E. Market St.
Passenger depot with general offices
Three-way turnouts
E. King St.
Coal ramp
Careva Machine Co.
Engine house
Home Furniture Co.
E. Princess St.
American Chain & Cable Co. (ACCO)
Prospect
Grand Ave.
To Delta Ma & Pa
Coal trestle   Scale   Yard office

A map of downtown York, Pa., shows how the Ma & Pa enters the city from the southeast, bends around the engine house near the main yard, then angles northwest toward the depot and a connection with the PRR.

Linden. NKP through-freight crews see the first car of this cut and stop to pick it up. (The traffic is too "hot" for it to wait around for the KC Local to pick up but once per day.) They only get the first half dozen or so cars, because I put a pin in the knuckle of the cut's last car to hold it open.

As the NKP picks up the first cut, a Circuitron optical detector is uncovered, triggering a Circuitron relay that turns on the power to the Monon unit. It creeps forward until the lead car of the second cut rolls slowly into view and covers the photo cell, turning off the Monon unit—and so on until all of the cuts of cars are delivered and the diesel sits atop the detector.

Now that we've examined the LDE selection process in some detail at Linden, let's look at a few more town candidates before discussing junctions.

York on the Ma & Pa
Stan White models the Maryland & Pennsylvania Railroad, a short line that railroad author George Hilton aptly described as a 12"-scale model railroad. Stan's HO railroad depicts key parts of the city of York, Pa. (fig. 2-8), as well as several other towns along the line.

The map of central York (fig. 2-10) shows how the Maryland & Pennsylvania's main line up from Baltimore entered the city from the southeast, then turned west to reach

their yard and engine terminal. The main made a hard turn to the north around the engine house (fig. 2-9), threaded the gap between the machine company and the sprawling American Chain and Cable Co., and then continued northwest across Broad Street to the depot on E. Market Street (fig. 2-11).

Finally, it continued northwest past the New York Wire Cloth plant toward a connection with the Pennsylvania RR at York Tower near the intersection of Queen, North, and York streets.

What's really impressive is that Stan managed to compress York's classic depot scene, engine terminal (shown in Chapter 6), yard, and several "signature"

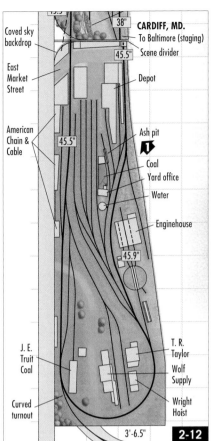

▲ Why the Ma & Pa was deemed especially modelgenic, even in its urban environs, is evident from this photo by Al Rung of gas-electric 61 heading east from the Ma & Pa depot (at left) in York, Pa.

industries into a Layout Design Element that fits on a shelf only 42½" wide! As Stan's track plan (fig. 2-12) shows, he did this by bending the curve past the engine house into a full 180-degree turnback curve. Comparing the model and prototype photos leaves no doubt as to what Stan was modeling. (A full report on Stan's HO layout appears in the December 2005 issue of *Model Railroader*.)

Selecting York is an easy LDE choice for anyone modeling the Ma & Pa. But York could also serve as a template for freelancers who want to model an Eastern short line that clearly embraces the distinctive architectural styles of the southeastern part of the Keystone State. Why go to the trouble of reinventing the wheel when there are so many appealing prototypical examples to choose from?

▲ One end of Stan White's HO Ma & Pa included most of the key structures and scenes in York, Pa. Note that the "reverse loop" is not a loop at all but rather is a clever way to conserve space by folding the scene back on itself.

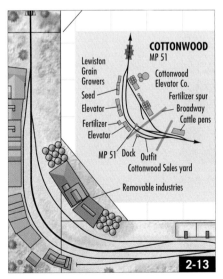

▲ The curve in the Camas Prairie's track arrangement at Cottonwood, Ida., made it an ideal candidate for an HO scale LDE that Dave Clemens fitted into a corner of his CSP track plan.

▲ This prototype photo by Dave Clemens shows how Cottonwood, Idaho, not only fits into a "corner" but also offers a row of tall structures that help hide the layout-backdrop joint. That's the Lewiston Grain Growers complex behind the train.

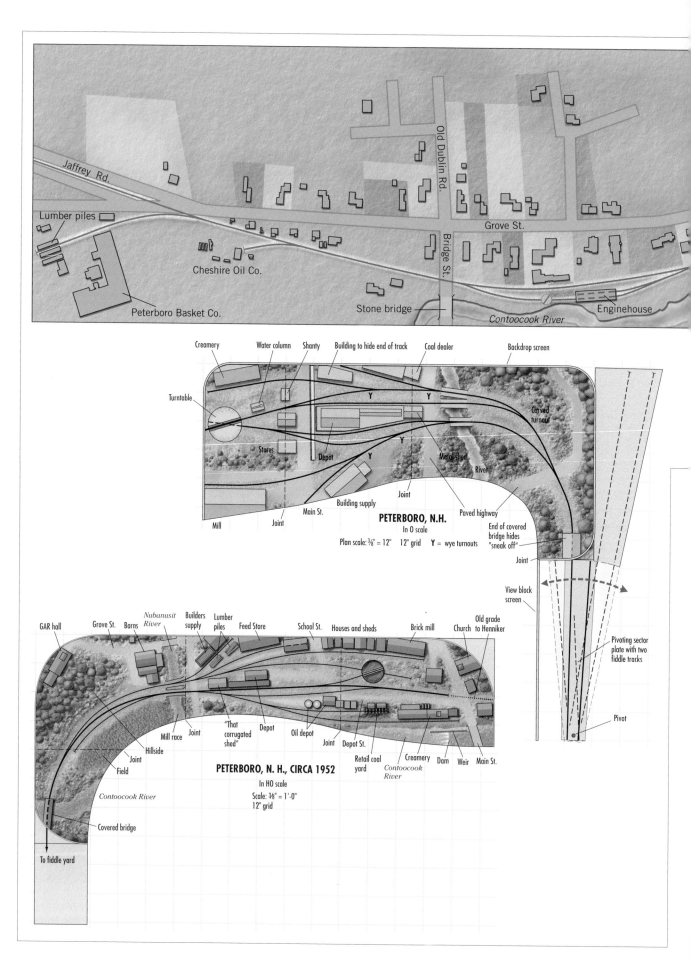

Jaffrey Rd.

Lumber piles

Cheshire Oil Co.

Peterboro Basket Co.

Old Dublin Rd.

Grove St.

Bridge St.

Stone bridge

Enginehouse

Contoocook River

Creamery Water column Shanty Building to hide end of track Coal dealer Backdrop screen

Turntable

Y Y

Curved turnout

Stores

Depot

Y

Metal shed

River

Y

Joint

Mill

Joint

Building supply

Main St.

PETERBORO, N.H.
In O scale

Plan scale: ⅜" = 12"   12" grid   **Y** = wye turnouts

Paved highway

End of covered bridge hides "sneak off"

Joint

View block screen

Pivoting sector plate with two fiddle tracks

Pivot

GAR hall Grove St. Barns *Nubanusit River* Builders supply Lumber piles Feed Store School St. Houses and sheds Brick mill Church Old grade to Henniker

Mill race

Joint

Joint

Hillside

Field

"That corrugated shed"

Depot

Oil depot

Joint

Depot St.

Retail coal yard

Contoocook River

Creamery Dam Weir Main St.

Contoocook River

Covered bridge

To fiddle yard

PETERBORO, N. H., CIRCA 1952

In HO scale

Scale: ⅜" = 1'-0"
12" grid

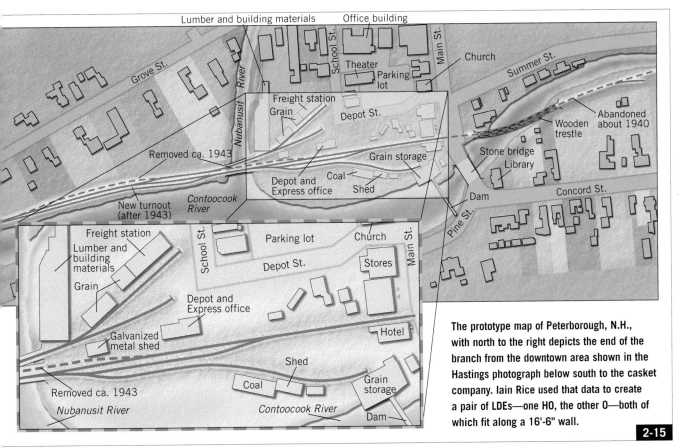

Lumber and building materials   Office building

The prototype map of Peterborough, N.H., with north to the right depicts the end of the branch from the downtown area shown in the Hastings photograph below south to the casket company. Iain Rice used that data to create a pair of LDEs—one HO, the other O—both of which fit along a 16'-6" wall.

2-15

Cottonwood, Idaho

The aptly named Camas Prairie RR in Idaho caught the eye of veteran track planner Dave Clemens. He reviewed the Camas Prairie's considerable attributes in MRP 1998.

I've picked Cottonwood, one of the several towns he converted from prototype track plan to Layout Design Element (fig. 2-13, page 17), as another good example of the LDE process. Here he needed a town that would fit in a corner, and rather than choosing an arrow-straight segment of the railroad, he noted that Cottonwood's built-in curve would fill the bill quite nicely. And the towering grain elevators (fig. 2-14, page 17) provide a way to screen the layout/backdrop joint.

We'll visit Cottonwood again in Chapter 10 as we use it and several other LDEs to design an HO layout.

Peterborough, N.H.

One of my all-time favorite railroad photographs was taken by the late Philip R. Hastings at Peterborough (also spelled "Peterboro"), N.H. The town was once a stop on a Boston &

2-16

▲ This inspirational 1950 portrait of Boston & Maine branchline railroading in New Hampshire was recorded at Peterborough by Philip R. Hastings. The Mogul at left is working the industries while another waits by the depot for train 8118's afternoon departure.

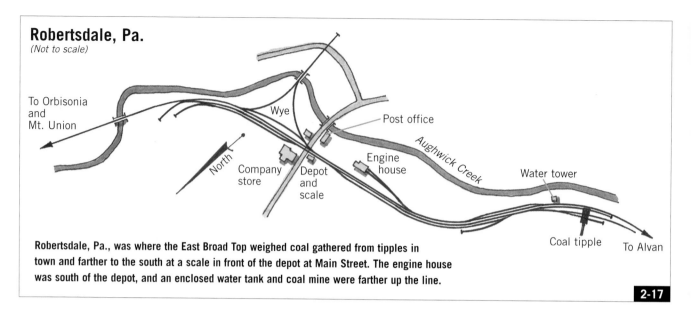

Robertsdale, Pa.
(Not to scale)

To Orbisonia
and
Mt. Union

North

Wye

Post office

Aughwick Creek

Company
store

Depot
and
scale

Engine
house

Water tower

Coal tipple

To Alvan

Robertsdale, Pa., was where the East Broad Top weighed coal gathered from tipples in town and farther to the south at a scale in front of the depot at Main Street. The engine house was south of the depot, and an enclosed water tank and coal mine were farther up the line.

2-17

Maine branch but became a terminal when the branch was washed away north of town in 1942. Phil captured a moment when two of the B&M's classic Moguls (2-6-0s) had paused in Peterborough with a local freight and a passenger train (fig. 2-16, page 19).

B&M's New Hampshire branch lines became famous because of their covered bridges and appealing scenery. As is evident in the photo, almost everything appears to have been selectively compressed to modelable proportions: modestly sized bridges and buildings, small trains and motive power and hence short sidings and runaround tracks, rolling terrain, and church steeples punctuating the skyline.

But what about traffic? Unless you operate by yourself, choosing to model a scenic line that supported but a single train per day often leads to layouts that gather dust. Fortunately, Peterborough's terminal status requires the locomotive on every train to be turned and serviced. This adds interest and takes time, effectively extending the apparent size and scope of the railroad.

As Randy Brown documented in *Model Railroad Planning* 2000, passenger train 8111 served Peterborough, then was turned to become 8118 after a two-hour layover. The local switched the line north to Peterborough, worked in town, and then switched what it missed going up the branch on the way back.

Iain Rice designed a pair of LDEs based on Peterborough (fig. 2-15, page 19), one in HO and one in O. Both fit in a modest area, feature the classic Hastings twin-bridges scene, and include most of the local industries and the needed turntable.

Other New Hampshire branches such as the Claremont & Concord line featured passenger service through rustic covered bridges (see Chapter 8). For prototype modelers and freelancers who enjoy modeling steam or diesel railroading of manageable proportions in a spectacular Northeastern setting, a careful review of the LDE potential of B&M's New Hampshire lines may pay huge dividends.

2-18

▲ William Moedinger, Jr., photographed East Broad Top train no. 3 with Mikado 17 by the depot at Robertsdale, Pa., just after it had turned on the wye. The Mike will cut off from the combine and gather up loaded hoppers before retrieving the passenger car.

2-19

▲ The enclosed water tank and a coal tipple were located well south of the depot at Robertsdale, where John Krause photographed one of the "big Mikes," 17, on a string of empty hoppers having its tender filled.

Robertsdale, Pa.

Hard to find even today using a GPS navigator in a car (as I recently discovered), Robertsdale, Pa. (fig. 2-17), was once a hub of coal-mining and railroad activity. It was served by the best known Eastern three-footer, the East Broad Top Railroad. The depot there (fig. 2-18) is now home to a museum operated by the Friends of the East Broad Top.

Robertsdale has most of the features that make a small town appealing as an LDE candidate. Coal mined in and beyond Robertsdale was brought here to be weighed on a scale at the depot. There was an enclosed water tank and small enginehouse (fig. 2-19) as well as a turning wye (fig. 2-20). Several coal tipples were right in town (fig. 2-21), so the coal bunkers of the EBT's six Mikados could be topped off.

As an LDE on a small freelanced railroad, be it standard or narrow gauge, Robertsdale is therefore an ideal site to model. Trains of empty hoppers could come up from the valley and be spotted at tipples. Loaded hoppers are picked up and taken back into town for weighing. When the local work is done, the engine can turn on the wye, be topped off with water and perhaps coal, and then head back down the valley to a coal preparation plant. (See Chapter 5 for more information on EBT coal operations at Mt. Union, Pa.)

Before it leaves, however, it may have to clear the main for a miners' or passenger train, perhaps a small steamer and two cars or, following the EBT's example, a gas-electric. It's hard to imagine anyone dreaming up a mountain town of this size that

▲ The wye at Robertsdale was just east of Main St. and diagonally across from the depot and scale at Robertsdale. This atmospheric John Krause photo shows a boxcar on one leg of the wye next to Mikados 17 and 16 in the railroad's waning days as a common carrier.

▲ This John Krause view near a coal tipple looks toward the enginehouse and depot at Robertsdale, Pa., as a Mikado chuffs past the depot through fresh snow.

In these mid-1970s photos, Spruce Pine, N.C., appears to be tucked into a "corner" alongside the Clinchfield (CSX) main line. Several industries are reached by stub-ended spurs.

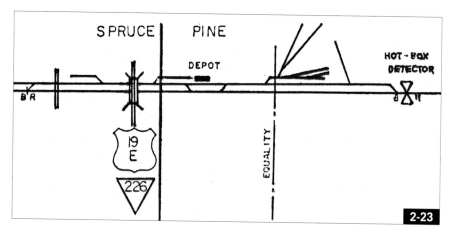

▲ This schematic from an official Clinchfield RR track diagram book shows the U.S. Rt. 19E overpass, depot, storage track, and lumber and coal spurs that extend "into the corner" at Spruce Pine, N.C.

▲ The NKP–IC crossing at Alhambra, Ill., was not a busy interchange point, as the rusty rail at left attests, but it still generated more varied traffic than a typical small-town industry. M. L. Powell took this photo on April 29, 1975 (J. David Ingles collection).

features more operation than an LDE based on Robertsdale.

Spruce Pine, N.C.
Room corners can be challenging to use creatively on a model railroad. If we ignore them operationally by filling them with scenery, we lose valuable real estate. If we run tracks back into them, it can appear as though we simply tried to stuff the corner with trackwork. Looking to the prototype for ideas is

especially beneficial when it comes to making plausible use of such space.

A good example of a prototypical use for a "corner" is at Spruce Pine, N.C. (fig. 2-22, page 21). It's tucked into a wide spot in the valley beside the Clinchfield RR (CSX) main line as it twists and turns along the Nolichucky River. Local industries (fig. 2-23) nicely fill the corner. The river bordering the fill that the Clinchfield was built on serves as an ideal place for the aisle.

The three stub-end spurs evident on the track schematic serve a coal trestle, a lumber storage area (perhaps for a nearby furniture plant) across Altapass Road, and (closest to the main) what seems to be a team track. Both north and south of town are feldspar operations. Feldspar rock is ground into powder for use as filler in paint, plastic, and rubber, but its principle use is in the glass and ceramic industries. It serves as a fluxing agent, lowering the glass batch melting temperature and helping to control the viscosity of the glass product. According to Clinchfield authority Steve King, that's where virtually all of the feldspar from Spruce Pine goes.

What appears to be a passing track isn't tied into the Centralized Traffic Control machine, as it is used primarily to store cars for local industries, notably the feldspar operations. Because the Marion–Spruce Pine job ran out of hours too many times (12 is the legal limit today compared to 16 in the steam era), a locomotive is often left at Spruce Pine to handle the switching, then put on a through freight and taken to Erwin, Tenn., for servicing over the weekend.

Alhambra, Ill.
I want to end this chapter on Town LDE candidates by segueing from Town to Junction LDEs, which we'll discuss in the next chapter. The "town" shown in fig. 2-24 underscores the premise with which this chapter began: Choose towns that have foreign-road crossings and interchanges.

As M.L. Powell's photo of the NKP–Illinois Central crossing at Alhambra, Ill., shows, the only key ingredients of a town plus junction LDE candidate are the crossing, perhaps an interlocking tower, and the interchange track, which—as here—is often one or two legs of a wye. A variety of traffic can be generated from one or two tracks without even building an industrial structure.

In that light, Alhambra, Linden, and similar towns that dot the nation's midsection should clearly be LDE candidates that rank at near the top of one's shopping list.

3-1

CHAPTER THREE

Junctions

Junctions—places where two or more railroads join or cross, where one railroad's main line splits, or where a branch line leaves the main—make excellent candidates for Layout Design Elements. As with Linden, Ind., and Alhambra, Ill., which we discussed in Chapter 2, a town LDE candidate may also feature a junction. In this chapter, we'll look at other types of junctions, starting with one at Cadosia, N.Y., where the New York, Ontario & Western's branch that tapped the anthracite coal fields in northeastern Pennsylvania split off the main (figs. 3-1 and 3-2, page 24).

▲ An aerial view of Cadosia, N.Y., where the New York, Ontario & Western's branch to Scranton, Pa., split off to the southwest from the main line, shows the depot within the wye, the engine-servicing facilities, and yards crammed up against Hawk Mountain.

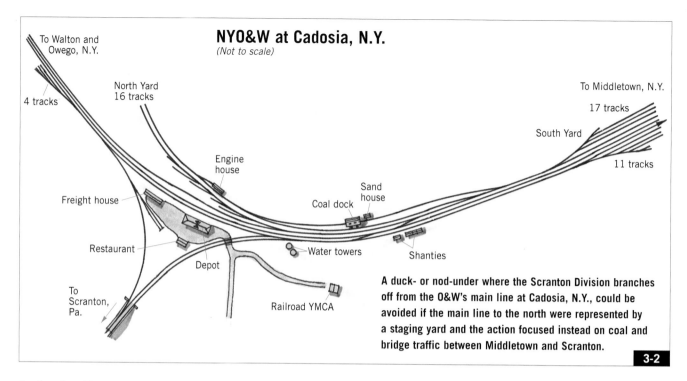

NYO&W at Cadosia, N.Y.
(Not to scale)

To Walton and Owego, N.Y.

North Yard 16 tracks

4 tracks

To Middletown, N.Y.

17 tracks

South Yard

11 tracks

Engine house

Freight house

Coal dock

Sand house

Restaurant

Depot

Water towers

Shanties

To Scranton, Pa.

Railroad YMCA

A duck- or nod-under where the Scranton Division branches off from the O&W's main line at Cadosia, N.Y., could be avoided if the main line to the north were represented by a staging yard and the action focused instead on coal and bridge traffic between Middletown and Scranton.

3-2

Duckunder dilemma

Before we look at Junction LDEs, however, let me point out a design concern: A line that crosses or diverges from another line can become an obstacle to the crews who are trying to follow their trains along the main route.

Paul Dolkos looked at this dilemma and offered some creative solutions in *Model Railroad Planning 2000* ("Railroad crossing solutions"), but there's no magic dust we can apply to our plans to make the problem go away. Keeping the benchwork high, thus creating a nod-under instead of a duckunder, is a good approach, as is curving the crossing or diverging line back parallel to the main route, thus avoiding a duckunder entirely.

Just keep in mind that creating a track plan that lets a person walk effortlessly along with his or her train should usually be a primary goal of layout planning.

Cadosia on the O&W

One of the more colorful, if not successful, railroads in the Northeast was the New York, Ontario & Western, usually called the O&W. It ran from the Hudson River through the Catskill Mountains to several medium-size cities in upstate New York. Until improving highways tipped the scales in favor of automobiles and buses, the O&W enjoyed a brisk passenger business during the warmer months carrying vacationers from Weehawken, N.J. (across the Hudson from New York City) up the West Shore (NYC) along the Hudson, then inland to summer resorts and camps in the Catskill Mountains.

If you glance at a map of the "Old & Weary" (fig. 3-3), you'll immediately notice that a major branch angles southwest into the anthracite coal fields of northeastern Pennsylvania. This line, the Scranton Division built in 1890, looks like—and in reality was—a "prop" for the rest of the railroad. Countless tons of hard coal were hauled up that

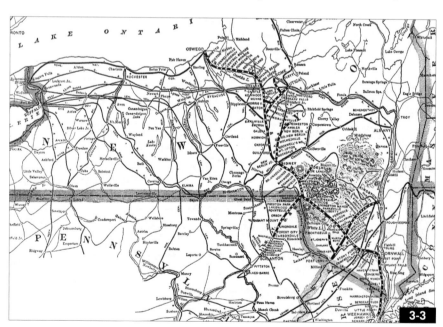

▲ This railroad map of the New York, Ontario & Western shows the main line stretching from the Hudson River at Cornwall, N.Y. (and over the West Shore to Weehawken, N.J.) to Oswego on Lake Ontario. Its most important branch was the line southwest from Cadosia, N.Y., to Mayfield Yard at Carbondale, Pa., and on to Scranton.

Bob Mohowski

J.A. McLellan

This trio of photos shows the variety of LDE types at Cadosia, N.Y. At left, a 2-8-0 on an NYO&W Scranton Div. local departs Cadosia for Starlight and Lakewood, Pa. in February 1940. Above left, a Mountain 455 pauses in front of the Cadosia depot (which still stands) in 1933. The photo above shows the small yard at Cadosia between Hawk Mountain and Cadosia Creek.

3-4

Robert Collins

division to Cadosia and beyond, mainly before the 1930s.

Cadosia was once a busy spot where coal trains turned east to head for the coal piers along the Hudson. Coal was also stored in massive piles here. I recently drove through this town along beautiful Rte. 17, which unfortunately obliterated much of the O&W's right-of-way following the railroad's abandonment in 1957. I was delighted to discover that the Cadosia depot still exists.

Cadosia hugged the south side of Hawk Mountain with the main line curving off to the northwest to Walton, N.Y., and east toward the headquarters and shops at Middletown, N.Y. The connection to the Scranton Division, which ran southwest into Pennsylvania, formed a wye that enclosed the depot.

The Scranton line had to leap across the Cadosia Creek valley to reach Mayfield Yard and the hard-coal fields around Scranton. The resulting deck-girder bridge that began at the turnout for the south end of the wye could similarly span an aisle, especially if some of the steel piers were eliminated or shortened to get more headroom for a nod-under. This would help solve the thorny diverging-route design problem.

(This is not the O&W's bridge over the Delaware River and the New York-Pennsylvania state line, by the way; that was three miles farther down the Scranton Division at Hancock, N.Y.)

Even so, the bridge may be a noggin-buster. You might therefore consider Ted Wetterstroem's solution to a similar bridge-over-aisle problem for his HO Chesapeake & Ohio railroad: He hung rope "telltales" from the ceiling on either side of the bridge, just as full-size railroads hung them ahead of bridges, tunnels, and other areas of low vertical clearance to warn brakemen riding atop cars to duck *now*! Lengths of soft rope brushing against your head would similarly remind you of the Cadosia bridge just ahead.

Building long and high bridges was something the O&W got very good at, since it cut across the corduroy ridges of the northern Appalachians, the remnants of huge folds caused by continental plates colliding hundreds of millions of years ago. The same continental crash heated and compressed the soft coal into anthracite, so it both helped and hindered the O&W.

Modeling Cadosia

Cadosia is an example of three LDE types in one: a junction, a scene, and a "town." Or maybe five: It also had yards and engine servicing facilities.

My perspective sketch, prototype track plan (drawn approximately to scale), and the several accompanying photos (fig. 3-4) show the major features that once graced Cadosia. Some of the most important were the water towers and columns (stand pipes). Eastern carriers were built in the early days of railroad construction when small steam locomotives were considered major power. Turntables were correspondingly short, as were roundhouse stalls.

As engines got larger, they consumed more coal and water, but designers had to cope with the length and weight limitations of the existing infrastructure. That's why tenders on otherwise modern steam locomotives on many Eastern railroads often were quite short.

The servicing area near the two water tanks on the O&W at Cadosia was a busy place indeed, as it served both Scranton Division and mainline steam locomotives. Although hard-coal traffic had petered out and traffic

As is evident in the June 1949 black-and-white photo by Richard J. Cook, the Mullens motor barn was home to the Virginian's fleet of electrics at the west end of the electrified district out of Roanoke, Va. The author's color photo from the mid-1970s marked the end of the reign of the ex-VGN Train Masters used in the yard between Mullens and Elmore, W. Va.

3-5

north of Cadosia had fallen off by the time the railroad dieselized in the late 1940s, the junction remained relatively busy. This was due to the Lehigh Valley connection at Coxton Yard near Scranton, which provided most of the overhead or bridge traffic at the west end until the end came in 1957.

The "main line" was by then Maybrook-Middletown-Cadosia-Scranton, Maybrook being an important connection to New England via the New Haven as well as to the Erie, Lehigh & New England, and Lehigh & Hudson River. Modeling Cadosia in later days as an LDE might therefore treat the southeast leg of the wye as the main, with the old main line to the north entering a hidden staging yard via a turnback curve or helix to a lower level. The south end of that yard could be visible, masquerading as North Yard just beyond the depot. That would eliminate the need for a duckunder to follow the line to the north, and southbound or eastbound locomotives could be held by the coal dock until ready for departure.

Cadosia's scenic location, wye and bridge, heavy traffic, helper service (trains faced a stiff climb out of the Delaware Valley), locomotive servicing, coal storage, "interchange" of freight between mainline and Scranton Division trains, and intriguing mix of locomotive types from Camelback 2-8-0s to handsome 4-8-2s and hulking 2-10-2 Bull Mooses, make it a good candidate for use as an LDE. It even originated a local freight behind an EMD NW2 switcher.

A railroad's economic viability and longevity are poor measures of its popularity with fans and modelers, and the O&W has been well documented in books. Many are out of print, but look for *NYO&W, The Final Years* by John Krause and Ed Crist (Carstens, 1977); two books by Robert Mohowski, *NYO&W Milk Cars, Mixed Trains, and Motor Cars* (Garrigues House, 1995), and *New York, Ontario & Western in the Diesel Age* (Andover Junction, 1994); and *The New York, Ontario & Western in Color* by Paul Lubliner (Morning Sun). William F. Helmer's *O.&W.* has recently been reprinted in paperback, and Manville B. Wakefield's *To The Mountains by Rail* can occasionally be found at swap meets and from used-book dealers.

Mullens on the Virginian

Another interesting single-railroad junction was at Mullens, W. Va., a hotbed of activity on the coal-hauling Virginian Ry. Making Mullens especially inviting as an LDE candidate is the combination of steam (or diesel) and electric locomotives that worked out of Mullens in the 1950s. The Mullens motor barn (fig. 3-5) was the west-end home of the electrics.

When I first visited Mullens and nearby Elmore in the early 1970s, it was the last place where railfans could watch the Virginian's hulking Fairbanks-Morse Train Master diesels at work. Electrification ended shortly after The Virginian merged into the Norfolk & Western in 1959, but the big FMs still shouted "Virginian" to us.

The Virginian's main line ran from tidewater at Sewells Point near Norfolk, Va., west into the bituminous coal fields. It passed through Roanoke and Princeton before heading north through Mullens to the Deepwater bridge over the New River east of the Mountain State's capital at Charleston.

Just south of Mullens at Elmore, a line continued west to a connection with the Chesapeake & Ohio at Gilbert, W. Va. Near the Mullens motor barn and depot (fig. 3-6), the incredible Winding Gulf branch sneaked out of Mullens by the back door, then twisted and turned as it played tag with the N&W on its way to Beckley, W. Va.

The junction, confluence of traffic from various coal mines, and engine change from steam to electric power for the climb toward the Virginia state line team up to make Mullens a fine candidate for the prototype modeler and freelancer alike.

Gerry Albers is resurrecting the Virginian, complete with the Mullens motor barn, in HO scale in his Cincinnati basement (fig. 3-7). He described how he used computer-aided drafting tools to design his railroad in *Model Railroad Planning 2005*.

Richard J. Cook

▲ Virginian train No. 3 pauses at the depot in Mullens, W. Va., on its trek west to Charleston. To the left of the Pacific is the motor barn and the branch to Beckley, which the highway sign says is 26 miles away. Richard J. Cook took the photo on June 18, 1949.

Gerry Albers is modeling the Virginian through Mullens in the years preceding its 1959 merger with the N&W. The precision of his CAD-generated track plan gave him the confidence to paint the backdrop and build a section of a VGN depot (to house the dispatcher's office) prior to completing the trackwork.

3-7

These mid-1970s color photos by the author show the Clinchfield's yard at Elkhorn City, Ky., at the north end of the railroad where it joined end-to-end with the C&O's Big Sandy Subdivision. The yard was squeezed between the river and the mountains, and coal tipples were located right in the yard. Just south of the yard is Pool Point Tunnel and bridge.

3-8

The modest engine terminal at Elkhorn City refueled both Clinchfield and Chesapeake & Ohio units from a tank car. The yard office sat inside the wye just north of a highway overpass.

3-9

► In the steam era, Elkhorn City boasted a pair of water tanks inside the wye, visible at left. The highway overpass had yet to be built in this July 1, 1947, photo by Floyd A. Bruner (C.K. Marsh, Jr., collection).

3-10

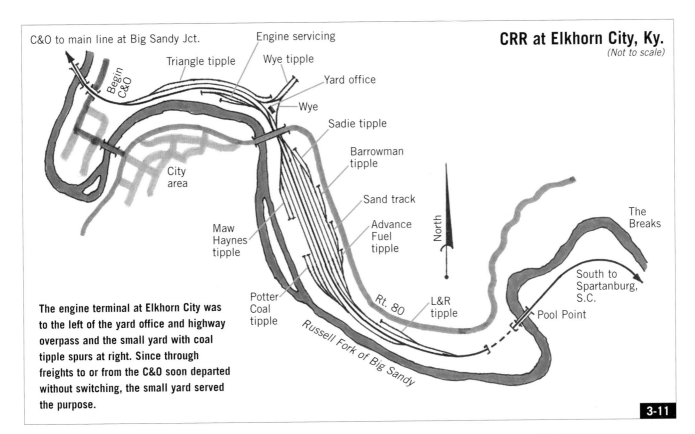

C&O to main line at Big Sandy Jct.

Engine servicing

CRR at Elkhorn City, Ky.
(Not to scale)

Triangle tipple

Wye tipple

Begin C&O

Yard office

Wye

Sadie tipple

City area

Barrowman tipple

Sand track

North

The Breaks

Maw Haynes tipple

Advance Fuel tipple

South to Spartanburg, S.C.

Potter Coal tipple

Rt. 80

L&R tipple

Pool Point

Russell Fork of Big Sandy

The engine terminal at Elkhorn City was to the left of the yard office and highway overpass and the small yard with coal tipple spurs at right. Since through freights to or from the C&O soon departed without switching, the small yard served the purpose.

3-11

Elkhorn City, Ky.

Deep in Appalachian coal country along the Big Sandy River is Elkhorn City, Ky., the junction where the southeast end of the Chesapeake & Ohio's Big Sandy Subdivision connected end-to-end with the north end of the Clinchfield RR. Today, the seam is invisible, as both railroads are part of CSX.

The Clinchfield stretched north from Spartanburg, S.C., past its main offices, shops, and main classification yard at Erwin, Tenn., and on up through some of the East's most spectacular scenery (including a tunnel with "portholes") to meet the C&O at Elkhorn City.

It seemed odd for a railroad as substantial as the Clinchfield to end with barely a whimper at Elkhorn City. The yard here (fig. 3-8) was modest, crammed between the river and the valley sides. The engine terminal (fig. 3-9) was even more modest; locomotives stayed here just long enough to find work on the next train headed back the other way. A wye, bent around a rocky outcropping and tucked into a side valley (fig. 3-10), allowed steam locomotives to be turned.

3-12

Aaron G. Fryar

▲ This photo by Aaron G. Fryar shows the Reading's outpost at Gordon, Pa., in March 1956, when the RDG's big T-1 4-8-4s were called back to service to push trains up to Locust Summit.

Coal was the lifeblood of the Clinchfield, and indeed coal tipples ("truck dumps") were located right alongside the yard here, as shown by the photos and several stub-end spurs near the words "yard office" on the CRR track diagram (fig. 3-11). But

the railroad also hosted a healthy dose of bridge traffic, including the hot Florida Perishable headed for cities of the Northeast with fresh produce from Florida.

This dual personality of coal hauler/originator and mover of time-sensitive

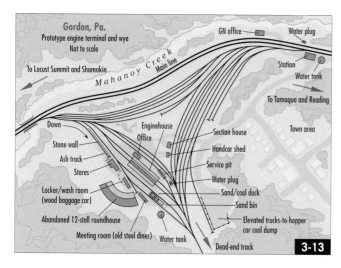

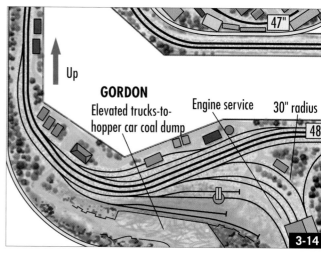

▲ Gordon, Pa., was a helper station and small yard located alongside Mahanoy Creek. The functions of the abandoned roundhouse and turntable were assumed by an enginehouse and wye.

▲ Jim Hertzog located the Gordon, Pa., LDE in one corner of his basement-size HO depiction of the Reading's coal lines between Reading and Newberry Jct.

overhead traffic makes the Clinchfield an attractive candidate for modeling or as a role model for freelancing. Indeed, it's not hard to "see" the Clinchfield when looking at Allen McClelland's Virginian & Ohio. And whether or not you're contemplating modeling the Clinchfield, Elkhorn City would make a fine candidate for an Appalachian LDE due to its narrow width and in-town traffic-generating potential.

Gordon, Pa.

Understanding what the Reading RR did for a living—hauling anthracite coal—is a lot easier than fathoming where it went. A map of the Reading doesn't exhibit the classic main-with-branches pattern of most railroads. But for those who took time to explore its myriad lines, rewards awaited.

One such crown jewel was Gordon, Pa. (fig. 3-12, page 29), located northwest of Reading along Mahanoy Creek. The roundhouse at this small but busy terminal was abandoned, but a wye allowed turning locomotives that

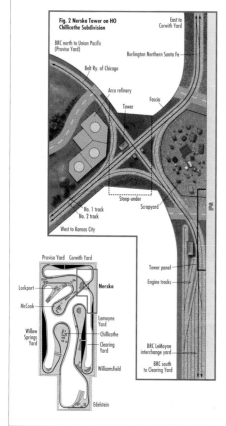

Bruce Carpenter built this simplified HO scale LDE based on BNSF's Nerska Tower near Chicago. The Belt Ry. of Chicago Alcos are heading for the UP's ex-C&NW Proviso Yard. Conflicts are unavoidable between layout operators following their trains and the benchwork at a major right-angle crossing like this. Bruce minimized the hassle with benchwork high enough to permit a "stoop under."

switched local mines and provided pusher service in both directions out of Gordon (fig. 3-13). A brick engine house and concrete coal dock tended to the motive power's needs. Train orders were handled at "GN" office at Gordon.

As Jim Hertzog explained in the 1998 issue of MRP, he featured Gordon as a key LDE (fig. 3-14) in a corner alcove of his sprawling HO Reading layout. Its intense operations and appealing structures make Gordon a fine choice for prototype modeler and freelancer alike.

Nerska Tower

In *Model Railroad Planning 2004*, Bruce Carpenter documented his busy Nerska Tower LDE, where the Burlington Northern Santa Fe's main line to Kansas City crosses the Belt Ry. of Chicago (fig. 3-15).

Bruce dealt with the inevitable problem of having one route through the diamonds block crews following the other route by keeping the benchwork high enough (60" from the floor to the bottom of the benchwork) to create a "stoop under" rather than a more problematic duckunder.

Bruce's approach reflects a general

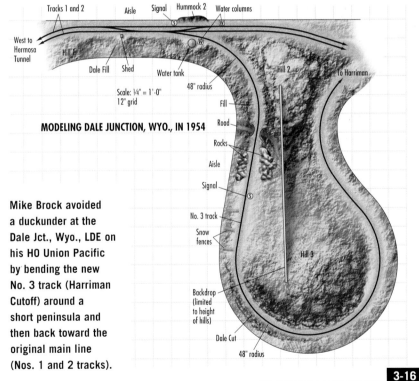

MODELING DALE JUNCTION, WYO., IN 1954

Mike Brock avoided a duckunder at the Dale Jct., Wyo., LDE on his HO Union Pacific by bending the new No. 3 track (Harriman Cutoff) around a short peninsula and then back toward the original main line (Nos. 1 and 2 tracks).

3-16

tendency to build benchwork higher. Whereas track elevations around 40" to 45" off the floor were once common, today designers more often opt for elevations in the 48" to 58" range. When you have to get under a segment of overhead benchwork, every inch of extra elevation is a plus.

UP's Dale Junction

The Union Pacific's busy Dale Junction in Wyoming is a scenic and operational highlight of Mike Brock's picturesque depiction of the UP in 1954 (fig. 3-16), as he described in *Model Railroad Planning* 2003.

To solve the diverging-route

Marty McGuirk modeled Essex Jct. on the Central Vermont as an N scale LDE but also drew an HO scale LDE for the same junction. Its distinctive covered train shed, wye, and myriad industries make it an excellent Junction LDE candidate.

dilemma, Mike looped the UP's more recently built Harriman Cutoff around a short peninsula and back toward the main line sooner than on the prototype. This allows operators following trains on either line to stay close to the action without the need for a duckunder.

Essex Jct., Vt.

Marty McGuirk chose Essex, Vt., as an LDE candidate for an N scale version of the Central Vermont Ry. The CV main line ran north from southern Connecticut before cutting northwest across Vermont to reach connections with the Canadian National at East Alburg, N.Y., and Canadian Pacific at Richford, Vt.

At Essex Jct., the CV had an 8-mile-long branch that ran west to Burlington, Vermont's largest city. A pre-Civil War train shed served as an acknowledgment of New England's often severe winters; Marty modeled it in N scale. He documented his rationale for choosing Essex Jct. as an LDE candidate in *Model Railroad Planning* 1998. The N and HO LDEs he designed for this junction are shown alongside the prototype's track arrangement in fig. 3-17.

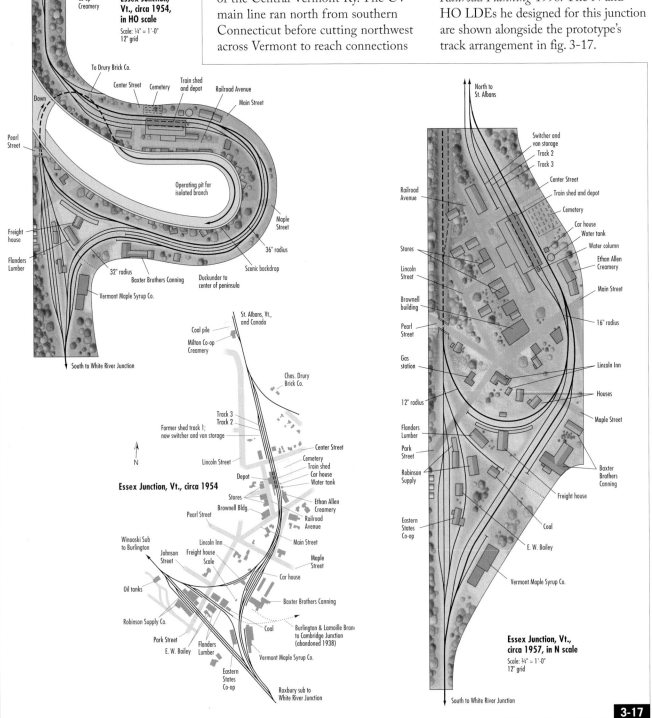

Essex Junction, Vt., circa 1954, in HO scale
Scale: ¼" = 1'-0"
12" grid

North to St. Albans
Milton Co-op Creamery
To Drury Brick Co.
Center Street
Cemetery
Train shed and depot
Railroad Avenue
Main Street
Down
Pearl Street
Operating pit for isolated branch
Maple Street
36" radius
Freight house
Flanders Lumber
32" radius
Baxter Brothers Canning
Duckunder to center of peninsula
Scenic backdrop
Vermont Maple Syrup Co.
South to White River Junction

Essex Junction, Vt., circa 1954

St. Albans, Vt., and Canada
Coal pile
Milton Co-op Creamery
Chas. Drury Brick Co.
Track 3
Track 2
Former shed track 1; now switcher and van storage
Lincoln Street
Center Street
Cemetery
Train shed
Car house
Water tank
Depot
Stores
Ethan Allen Creamery
Brownell Bldg.
Railroad Avenue
Pearl Street
Main Street
N
Winooski Sub to Burlington
Lincoln Inn
Freight house
Scale
Maple Street
Johnson Street
Car house
Oil tanks
Baxter Brothers Canning
Robinson Supply Co.
Coal
Burlington & Lamoille Branch to Cambridge Junction (abandoned 1938)
Park Street
E. W. Bailey
Flanders Lumber
Vermont Maple Syrup Co.
Eastern States Co-op
Roxbury sub to White River Junction

Essex Junction, Vt., circa 1957, in N scale
Scale: ¾" = 1'-0"
12" grid

North to St. Albans
Switcher and van storage Track 2
Track 3
Center Street
Train shed and depot
Cemetery
Car house
Water tank
Water column
Ethan Allen Creamery
Main Street
16" radius
Railroad Avenue
Stores
Lincoln Street
Brownell building
Pearl Street
Lincoln Inn
Houses
Maple Street
Gas station
12" radius
Flanders Lumber
Park Street
Robinson Supply
Eastern States Co-op
Baxter Brothers Canning
Freight house
Coal
E. W. Bailey
Vermont Maple Syrup Co.
South to White River Junction

4-1

CHAPTER FOUR

Industries

Choosing industries to model that are both visually and operationally appealing is a critical step in planning a model railroad. Ideally, the chosen industries will make interesting models and, at the same time, generate considerable traffic for the railroad. Moreover, they should help the viewer locate the railroad in both time and space. Appealing as a superbly detailed craftsman kit for a New England mill may be, the finished model will look odd in a Midwestern or Rocky Mountain setting. Communicating the purpose of the railroad to crew members and casual visitors alike will thus be much more difficult.

▲ The author's HO model of the bituminous (soft) coal preparation plant at Summerlee, W. Va., was kitbashed from Walthers parts. The prototype was fed by coal mined deep underground (hence the elevator shaft topped by bull wheels and hoist house at right) and by raw ("cleaner") coal mined on the C&O and hauled in over the Virginian— "loads in, loads out."

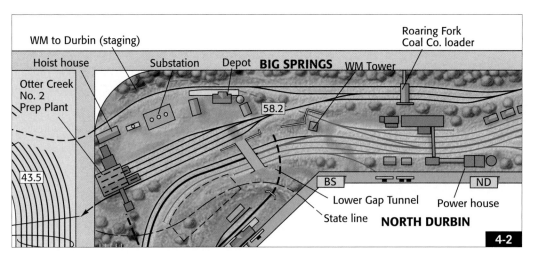

WM to Durbin (staging)
Hoist house
Otter Creek
No. 2
Prep Plant
Substation
Depot **BIG SPRINGS**
Roaring Fork
Coal Co. loader
WM Tower
58.2
43.5
State line
Lower Gap Tunnel
BS
Power house
ND
NORTH DURBIN
4-2

◄ The prep plant was located against a backdrop so that the empties-delivery track closest to the aisle could be extended through a hole in the wall. This allowed as many empty hoppers to be set out as there were loads to be picked up from the four load-out tracks. Each track was loaded with a single size of coal starting with "slack" on the right ranging up to "lump" on the left.

Coal in California?

What a railroad does for a living is greatly influenced by where it is located; a large coal mine in Florida or California would be as out of place as an orange-juice processing plant in West Virginia or Colorado. The prototype modeler's favorite railroad offers a closed set of industrial LDE candidates; the challenge is to select those that best reflect the railroad's regional industrial base.

At first blush, it would seem that a freelancer has an unlimited palette to choose from. But for those who want their freelanced railroads to evoke the plausibility of a full-size railroad, the choices of industries to model should mimic those of railroads in the locale and era the freelanced line depicts.

Wisely choosing a region and era to model is therefore a key to the railroad's visual and operational coherence. I've seen railroads that had superbly crafted structures, each a contest winner, yet the overall message was badly garbled. The builder simply chose structures based on their architectural appeal without regard to whether they complemented each other in time and space. What could have been an outstanding model railroad thus became little more than a series of unrelated dioramas.

Tools for the job

A railroad's industrial base also greatly influences its motive power and freight car rosters. The Illinois Midland and the Chicago & Eastern Illinois, for example, weren't Appalachian coal

haulers, but they originated considerable tonnage of southern Illinois coal, as their USRA 2-10-2s and fleets of open hoppers attested. Granger roads had endless fleets of 40' boxcars in the days prior to covered hoppers and often had locomotives that could tiptoe up and down light-rail branch lines to reach grain elevators; the Wabash's Moguls and the Milwaukee Road's SDL39s come to mind.

Freelancers can approach the decision of which region and era to model—and hence which industrial LDEs are appropriate—from several directions. If they have favorite types of motive power, they can pick the roster and then create a railroad that would logically employ that type of engine. If they admire a specific region of the continent, they can locate their mythical railroad there and let the example of other railroads in that region light the path of roster and LDE choices. If they want to model a specific industry, they can find full-size railroads that served it and base their freelanced railroad on one or more of them and the industrial LDE candidates it (or they) served.

Prep plant at Summerlee

Let's examine the industrial LDE selection process in some detail by reviewing one of the most interesting facilities I ever encountered on numerous forays into Appalachia. It was on the former Virginian Ry. (now part of Norfolk Southern) at Summerlee, W. Va. I didn't have an official railroad track chart for

Summerlee, so the HO model that I built for the Allegheny Midland (fig. 4-1, page 33) and track plan (fig. 4-2) were based on photographic evidence Jim Boyd and I gathered on field trips (fig. 4-3). The prototype had five tracks under the tipple; my model had four.

Summerlee was a combination deep mine and coal preparation (cleaning) plant. It was unique in that it served two railroads, the Virginian and the Chesapeake & Ohio, the latter indirectly. Coal loaded into Virginian hoppers was mined at Summerlee and crushed into marketable sizes. The "boney" or shale was removed before it dropped down through a series of ever-larger screens. "Slack" coal, also colorfully called "whiffle dust," was removed first and loaded into hoppers on the track closest to the vertical mine elevator shaft with the huge bull wheels on top. There was little market demand for this coal in the steam era, I'm told, so it could be purchased for the cost of shipping.

Coal was sorted into a range of sizes such as inch-and-a-quarter-minus. Often, descriptive names were used: pea, nut, stoker, steam, egg, and lump. (Unprocessed coal was called "run of mine.") Central Appalachian coal was bituminous, or soft, coal; the tectonic pressures that compressed coal seams, driving out the more volatile material to create hard or anthracite coal, were largely confined to northeastern Pennsylvania. (A handful of other sources of anthracite scattered across the continent resulted mainly from localized volcanic heat rather than the widespread pressure caused by the collision of the North American and African plates.)

The C&O also had a bituminous mine nearby, but no prep plant. They therefore delivered the "cleaner" coal to the Virginian at a small yard in Carlisle, W. Va., which was located alongside a signature structure of the coal fields, a brick company store (see page 59 of *Realistic Model Railroad Design*). The Virginian hauled the coal through Oak Hill and on to the prep plant at Summerlee.

As at any prep plant, the Virginian shoved empty hoppers via a bypass track to a holding yard behind the plant. As needed, those empties were fed to the several load-out tracks, each handling a specific size of coal starting with the fines close to the mine shaft. The Virginian also shoved the loaded C&O hoppers behind the plant where they were fed to a track that went under a car shaker, visible in fig. 4-3. (Coal tended to freeze in the hoppers in the colder months, making it difficult to unload.)

Once the coal had been shaken loose and dumped into the pit, it was then elevated on a conveyor to the highest point of the prep plant—the same point where coal mined underground at Summerlee was dumped into the plant to begin the cleaning and sizing process.

Coal started out as tropical rain forests when the North American continent was much closer to the equator hundreds of millions of years ago. Eroding mountain ranges buried the lush forests under a mantle of mud, eventually compressing the carbon content into coal. This didn't happen just once but rather as a series of tectonic events lasting millions of years. Coal therefore tends to occur in seams, each representing dense tropical forests separated and compressed by a covering of mud (eroded from a newly uplifted mountain range), which has since been converted to shale.

It is these intermediate layers of shale or boney that have to be removed from the coal as it is cleaned and sized. At Summerlee, the shale was carted away to a boney pile in huge dump

These two photos show the front and rear of the coal mine (note the elevator tower with bull wheels and hoist house) and preparation plant at Summerlee (also known as Loch Gelly), W. Va. It was switched by the Virginian, but raw ("cleaner") coal was also brought in from a nearby mine on the C&O. The car shaker behind the plant was used to unload frozen coal from C&O hoppers.

4-3

trucks; conveyors or even rail cars were also employed at some plants.

Up against the wall!

I used the LDE approach to layout design in several areas of my former Allegheny Midland RR, and Summerlee was one of those LDEs. On the AM, this prep plant was at Big Springs, W. Va. (fig. 4-1), named after a creek on a U.S. Geological Society topographic quadrangle map of the area between Hendricks and Glady where the plant was theoretically located. I had plotted the AM's main line from Dillonvale, Ohio, to Mountain Grove,

Va., on topographical maps, so finding appropriate place names was easy.

Unless one is prepared to build an operating prep plant that can actually dump coal into waiting hoppers, there is little reason to devote the vast amount of space required for the empties and cleaner-coal yard behind the plant. The main operational purpose of such a plant on a model railroad is to pick up the loaded hoppers in front of the structure.

I therefore located the prep plant against a stud wall, as shown in fig. 4-2. Only the bypass track actually penetrated the wall to reach a hidden

The AM tipple at Low Gap, W. Va., was kitbashed from Walthers' New River Coal prep plant to resemble the Republic Steel tipple on the C&O at Republic, Ky. Steel mills didn't require a variety of coal sizes, so only two load-out tracks ran under the tipple.

4-4

in Chapter 9, hence the term "tide coal." Other coal was routed to steel mills and power plants that rimmed the Great Lakes, hence the term "lake coal." Both terms were borrowed from C&O nomenclature.

The main lesson here is not to think of coal as a single commodity. This greatly increases its potential to add operating interest to a model railroad in that cuts of coal must be classified, just as boxcars and tank cars and flat cars are switched into blocks and then trains in a yard.

An inspiring description of the process of moving coal to market titled "Tide 470" by former *Trains* magazine editor David P. Morgan appeared in the April 1956 issue. Photocopies are available for a small fee from Kalmbach's Customer Sales and Service Dept. (1-800-533-6644; customerservice@kalmbach.com).

Modeling the prep plant

The versatile New River Mining Co. coal preparation plant kit from Walthers, available in HO and N scales, provided the fodder for this plant. I used the walls from several kits to kitbash the main structure. I sized the structure to make best use of the kit parts, but I tried to copy the shapes of the various parts of the prototype. The unseen backside wasn't finished.

I scratchbuilt the elevator hoist tower from Plastruct shapes. The hoist house was modified from a Pikestuff auto repair shop kit, as was a nearby maintenance shop. The electric substation was modified from a Walthers kit that's a bit too modern for this plant but looks okay when weathered.

The hoist cables to the elevator were elastic cords connected over the bull wheels (salvaged from a German mine kit, as I recall) to a weight in the elevator shaft that kept them taut.

Areas around coal mines are filthy, so heavy weathering was mandatory. I scribed the seam lines for the corrugated sheet metal panels, painted the structure Polly Scale SP Lettering Gray, let it dry, then rewetted its entire surface. I touched a brush filled with Polly Scale black to the top of each

panel and let the black wash down. When it encountered a seam, it spread out just as real coal dust would do when washed by rain. Touches of Rail Brown and Roof Brown added a touch of rust here and there, but signs of decay can easily be overdone in a working tipple.

More visual "texture" was added by cutting the window "glass" into thirds, then trimming the center section to its frame dimensions and gluing it at an open angle.

Switching the prep plant

Each morning on the Allegheny Midland, the Otter Creek Shifter was called out of South Fork, W. Va. Its crew found their 2-6-6-2 Mallet ("*mal-lay*" but usually pronounced "malley" in the U.S.) on the pit near the engine house, checked with the yardmaster to see which yard track their trains of empties was on, coupled to the train, pumped up the air line to release the brakes, tested the brakes, and got their Clearance Form A authorizing them to occupy the Centralized Traffic Controlled main line. At the dispatcher's bidding, they headed southbound up Cheat River Grade.

At Big Springs Jct., they picked up more empty hoppers that a northbound through train had left there for them, then at the junction switch headed onto the Otter Creek Subdivision and picked up train orders for this "dark" (unsignaled) branch at BJ Cabin.

After a tough pull out of the Otter Creek valley, they arrived at Big Springs, ran around their train, and shoved the empties into the bypass track. The number of empties shoved into that one track had to equal the number of loads picked up from the four tracks under the prep plant. That's why the bypass track extended through a hole in the backdrop and stud wall.

Five or six loaded hoppers on four tracks under and in front of the tipple meant that the staging track had to hold 20-plus empties. Had the backdrop wall been an outside concrete wall, I would have located the empties track along the inside of the wall under a mountain ridge.

staging track. Four load-out tracks were located under and in front of the plant where the Otter Creek Shifter's crew could pick up loads.

Each track contained cars loaded with a specific size of coal. For car-routing purposes, each track was essentially a different industry, as cars loaded on it went to a distinct destination. Steam coal, for example, was used in the fireboxes of the AM's steam fleet. Stoker coal was forwarded to coal yards for use in home furnaces. A lot of the coal was sent southeast to tidewater ports for export, as discussed

Once the empties were shoved alongside the tipple, the Mallet cut off and picked up the loads. It then picked up its caboose and got orders and a clearance form to head back down the branch to Big Springs Jct. There it set out any southbound tide coal loads before proceeding under CTC signal indications back to South Fork with its northbound lake coal loads.

Between operating sessions, I had two choices: I could remove all of the coal loads and put them in the empty hoppers that headed north or south into staging yards that simulate connections to other railroads. Or I could simply enjoy running the railroad for a few hours by myself as I returned the loads to the various tipples and moved the empties into the north- and south-end staging yards.

The logistics of removing loads of various coal sizes and matching them to a wide variety of empty hopper types would have been nightmarish, so I chose the latter approach. By running several such trains the length of the railroad, I was able to spot maintenance concerns that crews hadn't reported.

It's there if you look!

The several candidates for industrial LDEs discussed in the following pages are but a tiny sampling of the model-worthy candidates to be found in even the most cursory study of full-size railroads. With the almost limitless facilities we now have at our fingertips for doing research on the Internet, it is easier to find something that existed and condense it slightly, or a lot, to fit our modeling needs than it is to create a totally freelanced structure or scene. By choosing an actual industry to model in whole or in part, we sidestep most of the myriad opportunities to err based on a lack of knowledge.

Other industrial LDEs

Now that we've reviewed how a coal prep plant can serve as the basis for a Layout Design Element for a prototype (VGN) or freelanced (AM) railroad, let's look at two more coal tipples as well as other types of industries from various regions of North America that could make excellent LDEs.

"Truck-dump" tipples ranged from simple ramps above a depressed track to elaborate conveyor systems that elevated the coal after it was weighed. The author's HO model, kitbashed from an Accurail/Rix road overpass, is based on an East Broad Top tipple.

4-5

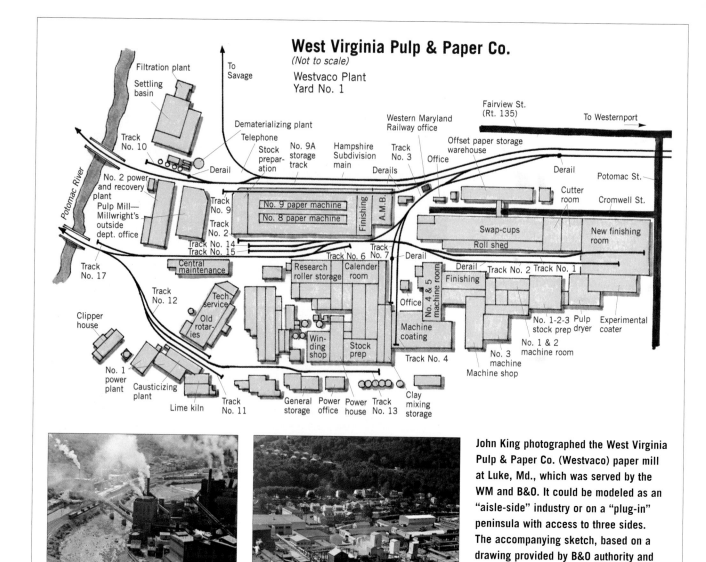

West Virginia Pulp & Paper Co.
(Not to scale)

Westvaco Plant
Yard No. 1

Filtration plant
Settling basin
To Savage
Potomac River
Track No. 10
Dematerializing plant
Telephone
Stock preparation
No. 9A storage track
Hampshire Subdivision main
Track No. 3
Derails
Fairview St. (Rt. 135)
To Westernport
Western Maryland Railway office
Offset paper storage warehouse
Office
Derail
Potomac St.
No. 2 power and recovery plant
Pulp Mill— Millwright's outside dept. office
Derail
Track No. 9
Track No. 2
No. 9 paper machine
No. 8 paper machine
Finishing
A.M.B.
Cutter room
Cromwell St.
Swap-cups
Roll shed
New finishing room
Track No. 14
Track No. 15
Track No. 6
Track No. 7
Derail
Derail
Track No. 2
Track No. 1
Track No. 17
Central maintenance
Research roller storage
Calender room
No. 4 & 5 machine room
Finishing
Track No. 12
Tech. service
Old rotaries
Office
Machine coating
No. 1-2-3 Pulp stock prep dryer
Experimental coater
Clipper house
Winding shop
Stock prep
Track No. 4
No. 1 & 2 machine room
No. 3 machine
No. 1 power plant
Causticizing plant
Lime kiln
Track No. 11
General storage
Power office
Power house
Track No. 13
Clay mixing storage
Machine shop

John King photographed the West Virginia Pulp & Paper Co. (Westvaco) paper mill at Luke, Md., which was served by the WM and B&O. It could be modeled as an "aisle-side" industry or on a "plug-in" peninsula with access to three sides. The accompanying sketch, based on a drawing provided by B&O authority and modeler Henry Freeman, shows key tracks and structures within the mill as of 1981.

4-6

Appalachia and the South

Not all prep plants have five or more tracks under them. A tipple at Republic, Ky. (fig. 4-4, page 36), fed by a conveyor that went over a ridge to a mine, was owned by Republic Steel. They needed only one or two sizes of coal for the steel-making process, so the tipple had only a pair of tracks under it. I kitbashed a model of this tipple again using Walthers' New River Coal kits; this model was described in more detail on page 80 of the October 1998 issue of *Model Railroader* in my series on modeling a coal branch.

Other coal tipples were simply truck dumps of various degrees of sophistication. Fig. 4-5 (page 37) shows truck dumps that could serve as industrial LDE candidates for modelers who don't have room for a prep plant, or who want to take run-of-mine coal loads from truck dumps to a prep plant for processing.

Another signature industry in Appalachia is the paper mill (fig. 4-6). Most paper mills convert pulpwood or wood chips into various types of paper. Some paper mills use chemicals to dissolve wood into long fibers, thus producing not only a distinctive aroma but also a coarser and stronger product such as kraft paper, used to make cardboard. Mills that employ mechanical means to crush wood into fibers produce finer paper, but it's not

as strong. Kaolin (white clay) is often used as a coating on fine paper to produce an "enameled" finish.

Rather than devoting a large area to a Westvaco paper mill at North Durbin, W. Va., on the Allegheny Midland, I modeled only a few buildings (fig. 4-7). Then I added long lead tracks that were truncated at the edge of the benchwork to suggest they continued on into this "aisle-side" industry. Crews still had to switch cars for the unmodeled part of the mill by following a diagram that showed the spot order of each type of car within the mill. It was not based on an actual mill and therefore was not a Layout Design Element (it should have

▲ To save space, the author's freelanced HO model of a Westvaco paper mill was an "aisle-side" industry—most of the mill structures were assumed to be out in the aisle. The unmodeled part of the mill was served by two long leads where outbound and inbound cars could be spotted. It was switched by a Western Maryland crew, thus adding another assignment (the "Mill Job") to each operating session.

Paper mills are located close to ready supplies of wood suitable for use in making pulp. This wood may be shipped to mills in the form of wood chips, shown being loaded on the Western Maryland at Laurel Bank, W. Va. It may also be shipped as pulpwood, as the photo by Mike Dodd taken in 1992 at Raleigh, N.C., shows (above, left). Pulpwood is transported on special bulkhead flats such as the ones the author photographed on the original Norfolk Southern in 1973 (above, right).   **4-8**

been!), but the same principles apply.

The operating potential of a paper mill is considerable. Pulpwood and/or wood chips (fig. 4-8) are shipped in. The mill may also receive carloads of kaolin as well as chlorine to bleach the paper. Coal or fuel oil may also be shipped in. Outbound are boxcar loads of paper or cardboard.

Thanks to nearby forests, Appalachia—as well as the Northeast, Pacific Northwest, upper Midwest, and Canada—are dotted with paper mills. Although they tend to be large, it's possible to model a paper mill in a reasonable space as an LDE. Walthers makes a plastic kit for a modern mill. Older mills tended to be a motley collection of brick and corrugated metal buildings plus an assortment of large storage tanks and piping.

Below the Mason-Dixon Line there is ample evidence of the lumber industry, including ancillary enterprises, such as furniture factories. There were numerous timber-hauling railroads scattered throughout the mountains, and they fed large sawmills such as the one at Cass, W. Va. (fig. 4-9, page 40).

Another large sawmill was located right next to a furniture plant on the Graham County RR in North Carolina, which operated a Shay and then a GE 70-tonner. The respective owners reportedly didn't get along,

however, so the furniture plant had its lumber shipped in by rail. The sawmill also shipped furniture-grade lumber via the GC and Southern to markets all over the country, and on at least one documented occasion one of the loaded flat cars wound up coming right back almost to where it started to supply the furniture factory! Only local railroad management noticed the irony—and got paid both originating and terminating freight charges.

An unusual industry to consider for an industrial or town LDE was a mica processing plant on the Clinchfield (CSX) at Kona, N. C. (fig. 4-10, page 40). It looks much like a concrete grain elevator or soybean processing plant. Mica, which is found as sheets, flakes, and scrap (smaller than either), can be processed into ground or powdered mica.

According to Steve King, author of *Clinchfield Country* (Old Line Graphics, 1988), the principal use for ground mica is in gypsum wallboard joint compound. Mica is also used in the paint industry as a pigment extender, he explained; the ground mica reduces chalking and prevents shearing of the paint film.

Ground mica is also used in the well-drilling industry as an additive to drilling "mud," and it's used in plastics and rubber as an extender and mold lubricant for making rubber products such as tires. Sheet mica serves as electrical insulators in electronic equipment and dielectrics in capacitors; the insulators between armature segments of electric motors are likely to be mica.

Steve reports that the plant at Kona shipped 10 to 15 cars of mica

4-9

4-10

▲ Saw mills were a major source of revenue for the railroads. Lumber camps were often served by geared locomotives such as this Shay on the Cass Scenic Ry. in West Virginia, shown on a short trestle next to the huge saw mill preserved at Cass.

▲ Most of the mica produced in this plant on the Clinchfield RR (CSX) at Kona, N. C., was ground up for use in joint compound, paint, and drilling mud. A starting point for a kitbashed mica plant might be a Walthers' cement plant or ADM grain elevator kit.

per day—some sheet mica but mostly ground mica used in joint compound, paint, and drilling-mud use. The silos stored processed mica, much like a flour or coal processing plant.

Kaolin, a white clay used to give paper an enameled surface and to make porcelain fixtures, is found in abundance near Kaolin, Ga.

It used to be dried, then shipped in boxcars equipped with roof hatches, but today it's usually shipped as a slurry in tank cars. It's now cheaper to pay transportation charges on the heavier slurry than to dry the clay, and a kaolin slurry is needed in the paper-making process anyway.

The glass industry flourished in

West Virginia along the Monongahela River. Eric Hansmann described the industry along the Baltimore & Ohio near Morgantown in the 2001 issue of *Model Railroad Planning*. He included a bedroom-size HO layout featuring Layout Design Elements, including Seneca Glass (fig. 4-11).

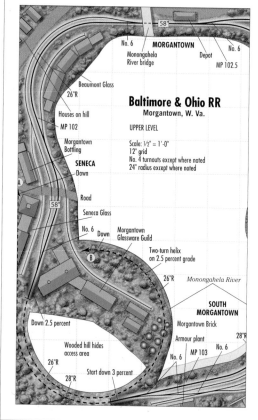

The Seneca Glass factory near Morgantown, W. Va., shown here around 1950, was used as the basis for an LDE on a track plan drawn by Eric Hansmann for MRP 2001.

4-11

A classic New England fiberglass mill near Boston—sprawled between the river and the railroad with company duplex houses lined up across the street—would make a great candidate for an industrial LDE.

4-12

New England

What industries do you think of when you think about the Northeast? A sprawling brick textile mill building along a river, perhaps with company houses nearby, immediately pops to mind (fig. 4-12). Thanks to a variety of kits, they're relatively easy to model and to enlarge by kitbashing into an entire mill complex as an LDE.

Another good candidate for modeling as an LDE set in New England is a granite quarry in Vermont (fig. 4-13). Granite results when magma slowly cools deep underground to form huge masses of solid rock with pronounced mineral deposits. It's later raised by subsequent mountain-building episodes and exposed as overlying rock erodes away. The collisions between continent

plates that shoved up the original and current Appalachians created plenty of opportunities for granite to form in New England.

The makings of stone structures from lowly curbs to lofty national monuments begin as thick sea-floor beds of lithified "sea shells"—limestone. This sedimentary rock is then changed into metamorphic marble by heat and pressure deep underground.

Slate is created in a similar process when shale is subjected to heat and pressure. Before quarrying and transporting marble or slate, we must first find old mountains, so locating a slate or marble quarry on a Midwestern railroad might raise eyebrows.

Other signature industries of the Northeast include paper mills (fig. 4-14), along with related industries

such as sawmills and lumber and pulpwood loading yards. It's hard to beat a paper mill for traffic variety.

In chapter 3, I included a photo of Claremont Jct., N.H. Just east of the junction was the town of Claremont, where the Boston & Maine's Claremont & Concord branch interchanged with the Claremont Ry. & Light Co. Together, the branch and street railroad later became the dieselized shortline Claremont & Concord. The electric railway and C&C served two paper mills, a shoe factory, a grain mill, a machine company, and a host of other industries that are characteristic of New England.

I built a large-scale (nominally ⅜" to the foot) "project railroad" for *Model Railroader* based on the C&C that was covered in several issues in the fall and

4-13

▲ The Rutland RR switched the Vermont Marble Co.'s quarry south of Danby, Vt. This December 1954 photo by Jim Shaughnessy shows the Bennington branch local preparing to move blocks of gleaming marble to the company's finishing shops in Proctor, Vt., located north of Rutland.

4-14

▲ This October 1976 photo by Ron Johnson shows a paper mill on the Maine Central at Madison, Me. In the '70s, the mill produced high-quality "super-calender" paper using kaolin as a filler rather than as a gloss coating. It received rail shipments of kaolin, wood pulp, "chemical pulp" in the form of "kraft" cardboard sheets, and fuel oil.

The author built a No. 1 scale (approximately 1:29) project railroad for *Model Railroader* based on the shortline Claremont & Concord. Inspiration came in part from Scott Whitney's articles in *Railroad Model Craftsman*, including his photo (here propped up on a power pole) of a 44-tonner rounding the tight curve by the Presto Grain mill in Claremont, N.H. Another LDE accurately depicted the trackage serving the Claremont Paper Co. two blocks south of Preston Grain; the freelanced mill buildings were kitbashed from a Pola roundhouse and Vollmer enginehouse.

4-15

4-16

▲ Small towns needed fuel for automobiles and furnaces, so unloading depots were often located at trackside. This one at Cayuga, Ind., shown in September 1971, was switched by the Nickel Plate Road and will be part of the Cayuga LDE on the author's HO layout.

winter of 2005. It was simply a trio of LDEs. One focuses on the Claremont Paper Co. near downtown Claremont (fig. 4-15), another on the distinctive Presto Grain building at a nearby street intersection where a line splits off toward downtown. I based the latter scene on an inspiring Scott Whitney photo in *Railroad Model Craftsman*. His coverage of the C&C and predecessor and successor lines appeared in the November and December 1993 and January 1994 issues.

The third LDE depicts a classic covered-bridge scene a few miles southeast of Claremont on what was once a Boston & Maine branch of the same name, as shown in Chapter 8.

The purpose of this series was to demonstrate that it's practical to build a large-scale, standard-gauge, LDE-based model railroad indoors. It also demonstrated the value of looking to the prototype as an example for even a small "switching" layout. No way would I have "imagineered" that diamond crossing in the middle of a busy intersection near Presto Grain or the switchback paper mill trackage!

The series also illustrates the importance of understanding the basics of prototype railroading, even if you're creating LDEs from actual trackage arrangements. To switch this paper mill, cars had to be coupled to either end of a steeple-cab electric or, later, a GE 44-ton diesel. Getting the cars on the desired end of the locomotive necessitated runaround moves, which in turn required a runaround track. But the nearest runaround was a few blocks to the south in a small yard I didn't model, so I had to add a crossover alongside the paper mill to accommodate runaround moves.

The central states

My new HO railroad is set in west-central Indiana and east-central Illinois in 1954. Then, as now, agriculture played a major role in its economy and that of the railroads serving it. In addition to grain elevators and lumberyards, towns had service industries such as gasoline unloading facilities (fig. 4-16), coal yards, lumberyards, and cement-block

Brickyards usually had one or more sidings where they received coal or fuel oil for the kilns and shipped bricks in boxcars. The brickyard near the Nickel Plate Road's St. Louis Div. main line in Cayuga, Ind. (top left), was managed by the author's father in the 1950s and today has the last coal-fired brick kilns in the U.S. George Berisso photographed a more modern Belden Brick plant in Sugar Creek, Ohio (top right), in 1993. The small brickyard at Lime Springs on the author's Allegheny Midland (left) featured Mr. Plaster pre-painted and weathered kilns and stacks.

4-17

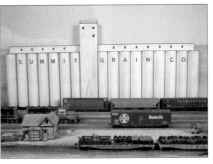

Grain elevators come in all shapes and sizes. Concrete elevators often had rectangular cores with rounded silos. These elevators were photographed along the Nickel Plate's St. Louis Division in Indiana and Illinois. Tommy Holt photographed David Barrow's concrete Summit Grain elevator, which nicely conceals part of the hard-to-disguise joint between the benchwork and backdrop behind it.

4-18

Limestone, metamorphosed into marble in New England, remained in its natural state in the Midwest. A major limestone quarrying region was served by the Monon and Milwaukee Road in southern Indiana, including this quarry at Oolitic photographed by Bill Akin. A key feature to include in an LDE would be a loading yard and building like the Ingalls operation on the Monon that Linn Westcott photographed at Bedford, Ind.

4-19

4-20

▲ Shoe manufacturing is often associated with New England, but there were examples elsewhere, including the Brown Shoe Co. in Charleston, Ill., once switched by the Nickel Plate Road.

plants or brickyards (fig. 4-17).

Just as coal tipples and company towns serve as signature structures on model railroads depicting the coal fields, other industries help the viewer to place a model railroad in another region or era. For example, grain elevators—the "sentinels of the prairies" (fig. 4-18, page 43)—strongly suggest a railroad in the flatlands between the Appalachians and the Rockies.

Grain elevators were originally wood structures, but many were later covered with corrugated metal siding. Others were concrete structures, often with a row of storage silos alongside. Their length helps hide the abrupt intersection of the layout with a nearby backdrop, making them good LDE candidates for their scenic as well as operating potential.

4-21

▲ A modern high-capacity printing plant such as this one in southern Illinois occupies a lot of acreage, but the rail-side facilities could be modeled in a reasonable space as a building flat against a wall. Such plants typically receive several boxcars per day filled with huge rolls of paper. Products are usually shipped by truck.

4-22

▲ The towering Swift soybean plant built in the 1940s at the west end of the Nickel Plate's yard at Frankfort, Ind., received strings of boxcars loaded with beans during the harvest season as well as hoppers of coal to power the boilers and tanks cars filled with solvents. As an LDE on the author's HO layout, this plant will cover a long section of backdrop.

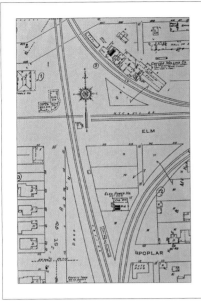

The now-abandoned electric light plant at Frankfort, Ind., was switched by Nickel Plate. If the plant ran short on coal, they would borrow some from the Swift soybean plant at the west end of town. Many small towns once had electricity-generating plants that would serve as LDE candidates, as is evident in the southeast quadrant of the NKP-Chicago & Eastern Illinois wye at Cayuga, Ind., on a Sanborn fire-insurance map. The map also shows the L-shaped depot, interlocking tower, and grain elevator complex, all of which are part of the Cayuga LDE being built by the author. **4-23**

All that grain had to go somewhere for storage. Chuck Hitchcock described the Santa Fe's huge Elevator A complex at Turner, Kan., in *Model Railroad Planning 2002*. He tucked a representative number of Elevator A's storage silos into an unused corner of his railroad room. By focusing on terminal operations in the Kansas City area rather than devoting space to a main line, he was able to replicate most of the trackage and functions of this and several other large industrial complexes and the yards that support them.

Other medium to large industries in the Midwest include limestone quarries (fig. 4-19), shoe factories (fig. 4-20), gravel pits that supply aggregate used to make concrete and to ballast railroad tracks, and clay-products plants that make pipe and roofing tile.

Larger cities had manufacturing industries that produced anything from automobile parts to paint. Gary, Ind., is famous for its steel mills, which require ship and train loads of iron ore, limestone, and coal. Huge power plants also use countless loads of coal. Nearby Whiting boasts huge oil refineries.

Battle Creek, Mich., is famous for converting grains to cereals. Those modelgenic "Ball Line" single-sheathed boxcars served the Ball glass jar plant in Muncie, Ind. Meat packing was and is a huge industry throughout the Midwest. Printing plants (fig. 4-21) receive boxcars filled with webs (large

▲ Canning factories were common throughout the Midwest. Jim Ostler photographed the Kemp plant near the NKP roundhouse and Monon crossing in Frankfort, Ind., in the early 1950s; this view looks west. (Photo courtesy Frankfort Public Library.)

rolls) of paper. Any of these could be "rationalized" into an LDE that forms the main theme of a model railroad.

Frankfort, Ind., a city on the part of the Nickel Plate that I'm modeling, has a sprawling soybean processing plant (fig. 4-22) that was built by Swift in the 1940s. An endless stream of bean-laden boxcars arrived at the plant. It also received solvent in tank cars and an occasional hopper of coal to power its boilers. It shipped soybean meal in

boxcars. Soybeans are an even bigger cash crop today, but as early as the 1940s they made a big contribution to the NKP's bottom line.

Frankfort isn't a large city, but it used to have a power plant to provide electricity to homes and businesses (fig. 4-23). Typical of many Midwestern towns and cities, it also had a canning factory (fig. 4-24) that initially canned local produce and later received perishables from out of state.

A car-repair facility is an excellent candidate for an "industrial" LDE, especially for freight-car modelers, in that a huge variety of both new and old freight cars are built, rebuilt, or serviced there. This C&NW photo shows the freight car shops at Clinton, Iowa. Built in 1956, it was designed to produce 1,000 new cars and repair 7,000 cars each year.

Before diesel engines were added to refrigerator cars, reefers had to be iced at intervals along the route to customers. This overview of the Nickel Plate Road's yard at Bellevue, Ohio, looking east shows the icing platform along the south side (John D. Burger photo from John B. Corns collection). An article about Bellevue appeared in the Sept. 2003 *Trains*, and the author's N scale track plan for a Bellevue Yard LDE (from the Sept. 2003 *Model Railroader*) is reprinted here.

Just as engine servicing facilities make not only excellent LDE candidates but actually serve as "industries" in that they require a variety of rail shipments to sustain (see chapter 6), car repair shops can serve as an industry that hosts an unequaled variety of rolling stock. The accompanying photo of the Chicago & North Western's car shops in Clinton, Iowa (fig. 4-25), clearly shows the many types and large quantity of freight cars typically seen near the shops. When it was built in 1956 on the site of the old Fifth Street Yard, the railroad projected repairs to 7,000 cars per year plus 1,000 new cars built.

Used in conjunction with a RIP (repair-in-place) track—another excellent LDE candidate, usually part of a yard—where running repairs can be made, a car shop therefore provides a "destination" for older cars needing substantial repairs or a point of origin for brand new freight cars to be picked up. As an LDE, it could therefore generate a lot of switching moves.

The West
Think of California and you immediately envision a string of Pacific Fruit Express reefers being loaded

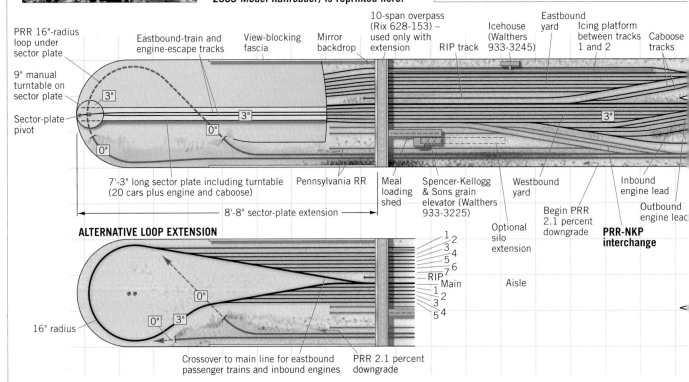

ALTERNATIVE LOOP EXTENSION

and then expedited to Midwestern and Eastern markets. The supporting warehouses, icing platforms (including those located in division-point yards along the routes to market, fig. 4-26), and unloading facilities would all make fine LDE candidates. Today, mechanical reefers make precooling, icing, and re-icing unnecessary, but the rush to get heads of lettuce and other produce to market continues.

The Pacific Northwest still generates carload after carload of lumber to build the nation's houses. Lumber once moved "loose" in boxcars; today lumber, plywood, and other building materials such as wallboard are often shipped in bundles on bulkhead and center-beam flat cars. The structures that support either end of the building material chain are well worth consideration for LDEs.

Canada

You may not think of a vast grain field as an industry, but it provides evidence of the economy of large regions of the U.S. and Canada. Model a small Canadian prairie town and you almost automatically get to model some portion of a wheat field (fig. 4-27).

Whether we think of agricultural

4-27

▲ Modeling a prairie railroad north or south of the Canadian border is largely a matter of selecting which grain elevator LDEs to use. Bernie Kempinski built this N scale scene in two 7' sections and covered the fields with trimmed craft fur; fake fur proved unsuitable, as the base fabric became visible when the fibers were trimmed to N scale height.

segments of our railroads as town, scenic, or industrial LDEs, it's important to allow space for them in the design of a granger-belt layout. A lone grain elevator will convey some sense of the local economy and the railroad's reason for serving it, but modeling the elevator without nearby fields and farms would be like modeling a port scene without water.

Incidentally, this is where those

who model in N or Z scale have an advantage. The distance from the aisle to the deep part of a scene shouldn't exceed our reach, about 30". Between the fascia and a single-track main line, that creates an HO scene perhaps 150' deep—not bad, but compare that to a scene more than 300' deep in N scale! Creating a scene of such scale depth in HO, let alone S or O, would create severe reach-in problems.

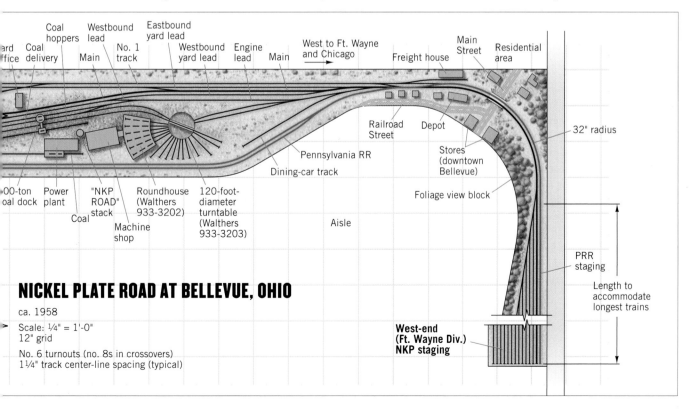

Coal hoppers | Westbound lead | Eastbound yard lead | Main Street | Residential area
ard ffice | Coal delivery | Main | No. 1 track | Westbound yard lead | Engine lead | Main | West to Ft. Wayne and Chicago | Freight house |

Railroad Street | Depot

Pennsylvania RR

Dining-car track

Stores (downtown Bellevue)

32" radius

Foliage view block

00-ton oal dock | Power plant | "NKP ROAD" stack | Roundhouse (Walthers 933-3202) | 120-foot-diameter turntable (Walthers 933-3203)

Coal

Machine shop

Aisle

PRR staging

Length to accommodate longest trains

NICKEL PLATE ROAD AT BELLEVUE, OHIO

ca. 1958

Scale: ¼" = 1'-0"
12" grid

No. 6 turnouts (no. 8s in crossovers)
1¼" track center-line spacing (typical)

West-end (Ft. Wayne Div.) NKP staging

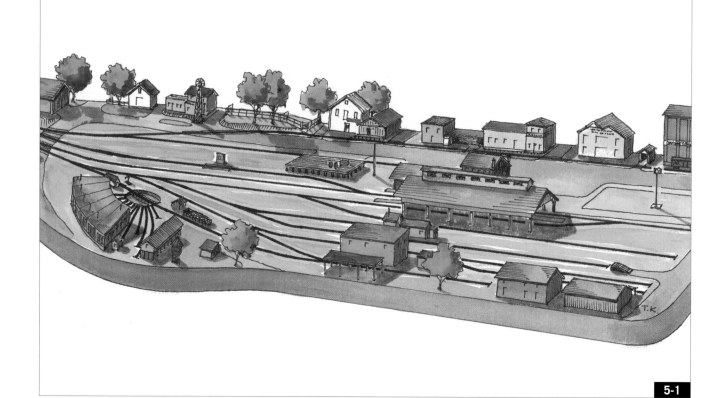

5-1

CHAPTER FIVE

Small and mid-size yards

▲ The small Pennsylvania Railroad (ex-Waynesburg & Washington) narrow-gauge yard at Waynesburg, Pa., looks like it was designed for a model railroad. Whether modeled in narrow or standard gauge, the yard has almost everything needed at one end of a branch or short line: small yard, locomotive servicing facilities, roundhouse, turntable, passenger station, and several industries. The river along the south edge is ideally located for use as an aisle, and the town structures make an ideal backdrop.

The term "yard" refers to an arrangement of tracks where cars can be sorted ("classified") into blocks and then into trains by destination. Yards also allow trains to be broken apart into individual cars or short cuts of cars for local delivery. Yards come in many varieties from huge classification yards at major terminals to small outlying yards that support a large industry or industrial park, or that provide a place where cars headed to or from a branch can be set out or picked up.

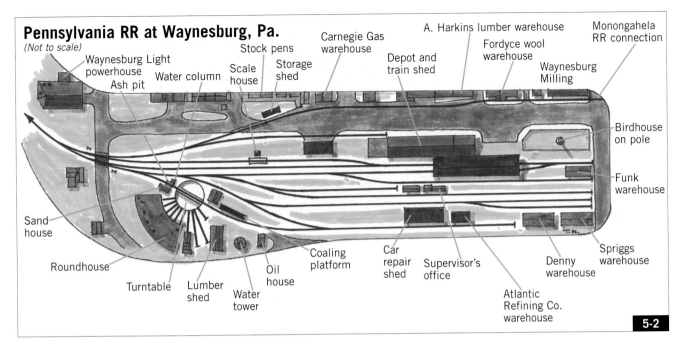

Pennsylvania RR at Waynesburg, Pa.
(Not to scale)

Waynesburg Light powerhouse
Ash pit
Water column
Scale house
Storage shed
Stock pens
Carnegie Gas warehouse
Depot and train shed
A. Harkins lumber warehouse
Fordyce wool warehouse
Monongahela RR connection
Waynesburg Milling
Birdhouse on pole
Funk warehouse
Sand house
Roundhouse
Turntable
Lumber shed
Water tower
Oil house
Coaling platform
Car repair shed
Supervisor's office
Atlantic Refining Co. warehouse
Denny warehouse
Spriggs warehouse

5-2

Understanding yards

This book is not intended as a primer on layout or yard design but rather focuses on using prototype examples to ensure better track plans. For background information on the design and operation of yards, I recommend Andy Sperandeo's book, *The Model Railroader's Guide to Freight Yards* (Kalmbach Books, 2004). One of my books, *Realistic Model Railroad Design* (Kalmbach Books 2004), provides an overview of design considerations for an entire layout.

After you review those yard and layout design tips, you'll then be better equipped to find a prototype yard to use as a specific example of a workable benchmark for your own yard. To help you get started, let's review several candidates for yard LDEs.

One caveat: Passive staging and active fiddle yards are also part of the mix on a model railroad. They aren't based on specific prototypes, so they aren't really LDE candidates. But it pays to treat them like LDEs when making "puzzle pieces" to move around on a scale drawing of the railroad room, as we'll do in Chapter 10.

Waynesburg, Pa.

The perspective drawing (fig. 5-1) and track plan (fig. 5-2) depict a Pennsylvania Railroad yard at Waynesburg, Pa. If it seems a bit

▲ This On2½ (¼" scale models running on HO-gauge track) LDE fits in about the same length as a typical HO yard, although the track spacing has been increased from 2" to 3". The resulting reach-in distance favors locating it on a peninsula. Narrow-gauge car and locomotive lengths are relatively short and comparable to late-steam-era standard-gauge equipment in HO.

small for something the sprawling Pennsy would typically inhabit, that's because it was originally built by the Waynesburg & Washington Railroad, a three footer. It came under the PRR's influence early on, and most W&W rolling stock and all locomotives got PRR paint and were renumbered around 1920. Mogul (2-6-0) No. 4, stored in a shed in Waynesburg, became 9684, for example.

Most yards are double-ended, but here's a prototypical example of a small, stub-ended yard. Its basic functions don't depend on it being narrow gauge; the track arrangement would work just as well for a freelanced standard-gauge short line or the end of a branch line.

The South Fork of Ten Mile Creek abuts the south edge of the yard, an ideal location for the main aisle. There's a handsome two-story brick depot (it lasted until the mid '90s), and the commercial buildings along First Street (fig. 5-3, page 50) make great candidates for flats along a backdrop. The main connection to the standard-gauge network was at the other end of the line in Washington, Pa., although the Monongahela RR eventually connected to the PRR here (an idler

flat was employed so narrow-gauge engines could move standard-gauge cars) and later continued through town on the track next to the mill.

My perspective drawing and On2½ (also called On30) track plan are based on photos and a plan that appeared in Larry L. Koehler's book on the W&W, *Three Feet on the Panhandle* (Railhead Publications 1983). Excellent scale drawings of most W&W locomotives and rolling stock, depots, and the Waynesburg roundhouse as well as town trackage arrangements are included in this inspiring reference. A more recent book, *Narrow Gauge in Southwestern Pennsylvania: The Waynesburg & Washington* by James D. Weinschenker (M2FQ Publications, 2003), includes a drawing of this yard as well as town diagrams and more photos.

Since the yard is stub-ended, inbound locomotives on passenger trains escaped using a runaround track. Inbound freight power could escape using a double-ended siding just west of the depot or a nearby crossover, then head for the roundhouse lead for turning and servicing.

The industries suggest the types of traffic that kept the W&W in business.

The author photographed the old PRR-W&W depot and commercial buildings along First Street in Waynesburg in July 1989. A shed straddled two tracks to the left of the depot. The roundhouse was located down the street behind the depot.

5-3

Freight was hauled in or on W&W flat cars, gondolas, tank cars, boxcars, two automobile cars, stock cars, and hoppers. The line had seven cabooses that ranged from converted coaches to four-wheel bobbers (1000 and 1001). Passenger equipment included an excursion gondola, head-end cars, combines, coaches, and even a coach-observation (no. 13).

Why On2½? Bachmann has produced a 2-6-0 as well as freight and passenger cars lettered for the PRR, an excellent starting point for those who maintain the narrow-gauge nature of this yard. Its O scale heft but HO track gauge allow big-time railroading in a modest area and on a modest budget.

Those of you who are used to planning yards in N or HO scales will

find, as I did, that reach-in distance becomes a primary concern. Starting at the top of the LDE track plan (fig. 5-2,), you can count ten tracks. If they were all spaced 3" (12 scale feet) on centerlines, typical for On2½ or On3, that puts the most distant track just inside the recommended 30" maximum reach-in distance. But several tracks have wider spacing to accommodate the street, depot, and some structures, and a buffer is needed between the aisle and outermost track. I therefore located the plan on a peninsula to allow access from both sides, something that wouldn't be needed in a smaller scale.

There was plenty of action on this slim-gauge railroad. W&W timetable 57, dated Sunday, May 25, 1919,

showed four daily eastward (actually headed north from Waynesburg to Washington) and four westward passenger trains; Sunday had two trains in each direction. Running time for the 28-mile trip was just under an hour and a half. Freights ran as extras, and it appears that four trains per day (two round trips) were typical.

The last scheduled passenger run was on July 9, 1929, behind 9684. The last steam-powered freight run was on April 6, 1933, again behind 9684. A railcar then provided service until the entire line was standard-gauged in 1943 and '44. One run between Washington and Dunn was made by a PRR B6s 0-6-0, but that apparently traumatic event wasn't repeated. The PRR built a railtruck to handle local freight, and the former W&W staggered into the Penn Central and Conrail eras.

A freelancer could postulate that his or her railroad picked up where the PRR left off in 1933 and continue narrow-gauge operations into more modern times under the original W&W banner. Perhaps the connection with the Monongahela at Waynesburg could have upped the ante enough to continue operations into the diesel era using Alcos and GEs based on White Pass & Yukon prototypes.

Change scales?
Thanks to a narrow-gauge railroad's tight curves and short trains, modeling a slim-gauge line is a good way to fit more railroading in a small space. But for those who prefer big-time railroading, let's consider another approach.

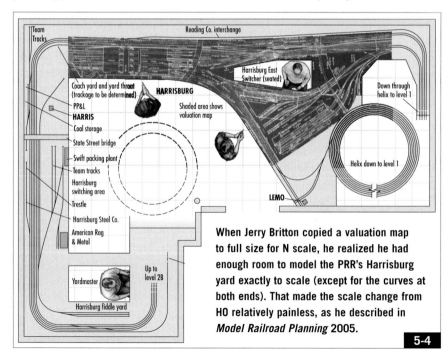

When Jerry Britton copied a valuation map to full size for N scale, he realized he had enough room to model the PRR's Harrisburg yard exactly to scale (except for the curves at both ends). That made the scale change from HO relatively painless, as he described in *Model Railroad Planning* 2005.

5-4

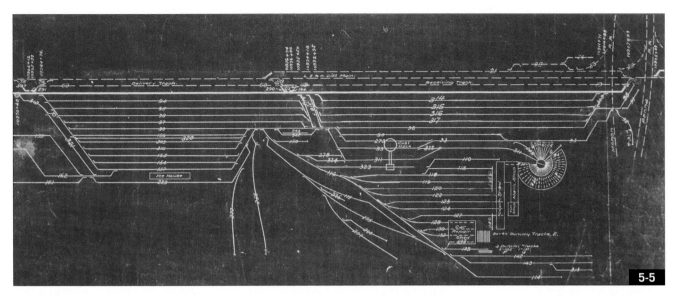

5-5

In *Model Railroad Planning 2005*, Pennsylvania RR modeler Jerry Britton explained the space problems he encountered when he chose to model Harrisburg, Pa., as a very large LDE. He was having a tough time figuring out how to cram Pennsy's yard into his basement when a fellow PRR modeler sent him a copy of a valuation map for Harrisburg.

The Valuation Act of 1913 required the Interstate Commerce Commission to determine the valuation of property and assets of every railroad in the U.S. Finished around 1921, the process resulted in maps covering every mile of right-of-way, so finding a copy of a val map is akin to striking gold.

Jerry realized that he could model Harrisburg yard virtually intact if he switched from HO to N scale, the only compromise being curving the

▲ Although not drawn to scale, the official track diagram for the NKP yard at Frankfort, Ind., correctly shows both east and west leads for the eastbound yard were relatively short. The Main Yard Lead, track 90, runs just above the coal dock and ties into the East Shop Lead (track 93). The West Switching Lead, track 312 at far left, connects the west ladder with the St. Louis Div. main line. Track 321 is the West Caboose Track.

approaches to either end of the yard (fig. 5-4). He was more interested in accurately depicting a favorite prototype location as an LDE than in sticking with HO, so he did some homework, liked what he found, and switched to N.

Another plus for the LDE approach to layout design and construction: Jerry was able to use the val map as a template for track laying after making a copy that was actual size for N scale.

Lead length
Before we examine other yard LDE candidates, I'd like to share something

I recently learned about yard design. One long-held tenet is that we need to provide a yard lead as long as the longest yard track so the yard switcher can pull an entire track as one long cut.

Handy as that sounds, it also points out a lack of understanding about how railroaders did their jobs safely. When I studied railroad drawings of the east end of the Nickel Plate's eastbound yard at Frankfort, Ind., which I'm modeling, I couldn't find a long yard lead (fig. 5-5). The busy Pennsylvania RR crossing and, to a lesser extent, the Monon crossing just east of the roundhouse limited lead length.

W. Clifford Cottrell stood on the River Road overpass to photograph the Rutland yard in December 1954 two years after steam's demise, but the wood coal dock remained. Looking southeast from the same bridge in June 1947, Philip R. Hastings recorded the arrival of "borrowed" B&M Pacific 3656 on train 65, the *Green Mountain Flyer*, from Troy.

5-6

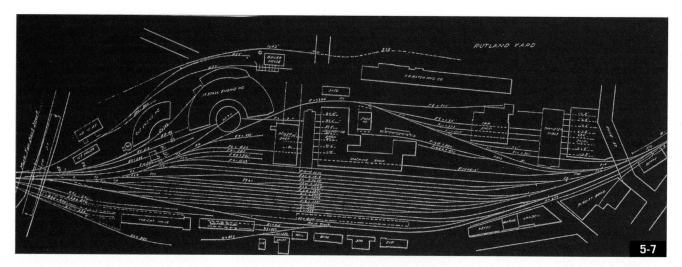

5-7

So how did the NKP pull an entire eastbound yard track?

When I checked with my good friend and advisor Don Daily, who worked out of Frankfort as an engineer for the NKP and successor N&W, he disabused me of the notion that the lead should be as long as the longest yard track. It wouldn't have been safe to pull an entire track filled with cars, especially in the days before radios,

▲ Rutland yard makes an excellent candidate for an LDE because of its compact size, natural backdrop of city buildings, engine-serving facilities, and the junction between two Rutland lines and Howe Scale complex east of the overpass.

Don cautioned. The engineer couldn't see hand signals more than 10 or 15 cars away as a cut curved this way and that along the ladder, so they tried not to handle cuts of greater length.

Pulling an entire track may have been done elsewhere, and perhaps it

can be done safely now that radios rather than eyesight are the primary means of communication, but Don didn't do it that way in Frankfort during the steam and early diesel era. Live and learn—and ask questions!

The Western Maryland yard at Elkins, W. Va., was primarily used to build coal trains from loads gathered up on branches to the south. A two-story brick depot housed division offices. The author took these photos in 1971 (looking railroad east at Alco RS-3s) and 1976.

5-8

► This WM schematic of the yard at Elkins, W. Va., shows four ways out of town, including trackage rights over the B&O to Bellington. Coal loads went to the right (railroad east) to Thomas and Cumberland.

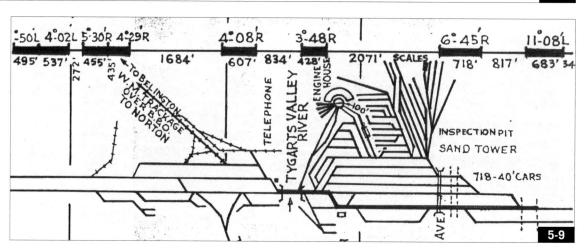

5-9

5-10

▲ To avoid getting coal ("whiffle") dust in the wood chips, chip hoppers were blocked on the head end of the Western Maryland's local out of Elkins. The author photographed the local in May 1973 as it commenced its daily struggle with the stiff Black Fork Grade east of Parsons, W. Va. (See Chapter 7 for an additional photo of this grade.)

Other yard candidates

Now that we've taken a closer look at two Pennsylvania RR yards at either end of the size and complexity spectrum, let's look at some other yard LDE candidates before turning our attention to engine terminals in Chapter 6.

The Rutland at Rutland

A fine candidate for a Layout Design Element based on a yard and adjacent engine terminal, with a junction thrown in to boot, was the Rutland RR's yard at Rutland, Vt. (fig. 5-6, page 51), which was the hub of the railroad. The Rutland RR was shaped like an upside-down Y with Rutland at the junction of the lines southeast to Bellows Falls, Vt., and southwest through North Bennington to a Boston & Albany (New York Central) connection at Chatham, N. Y. It ran north from Rutland to the Canadian border, then paralleled the border west to Ogdensburg, N. Y.

The River Street overpass at Rutland, seemingly built as a railfan's photographic perch, visually separated the yard and downtown area along the north side of the yard from the junction. Inside the crotch of the Y

The compact Huntsville (Ala.) International Intermodal Center is positioned between the airport runways and a small yard serviced by the Norfolk Southern. An Alco RS-1 handles car movements within the small yard. Its small size makes it an excellent candidate for conversion to an LDE. The aerial photo was supplied by the Huntsville International Intermodal Center.

5-11

was Howe Scale Co., itself an excellent LDE candidate.

The cityscape along the north edge of the yard, evident in the railroad's plan view of the yard (fig. 5-7), would form a great background flat. Conversely, the engine terminal and roundhouse are on the aisle side of the yard, forcing yard crews to work around them. As long as they have access to the throats, they should be okay.

At the turn of the century, a dozen passenger and mixed trains were scheduled in or out of Rutland each day. By the century's mid-point, passenger service was gone.

Even though Rutland was a one-railroad town, Boston & Maine power came up the Bennington Branch on no. 65, the New York section of the Green Mountain Flyer, as shown in fig. 5-6. This resulted from the Rutland using B&M trackage to reach Troy, N. Y., and the need to balance mileage.

A careful choice of LDE candidate may therefore allow trains or motive power from two or more railroads to be modeled. The freelancer can similarly operate trains from a prototypical railroad alongside those of his or her freelanced line, thus helping to ensure that viewers readily grasp the mythical railroad's locale and era.

The Rutland was one of the first railroads to dieselize as Alco RS-1s and RS-3s arrived on the property in the early 1950s. Its green-and-yellow Pullman-Standard PS-1 boxcars and extended-vision-cupola cabooses gave it a modern look despite the company's declining fortunes.

It was abandoned in 1962 following a lengthy management-labor impasse. Portions of the railroad were taken over by the Green Mountain Ry. and the Vermont Ry. and continue to operate to this day, including the line past the Howe Scale Co. into Rutland.

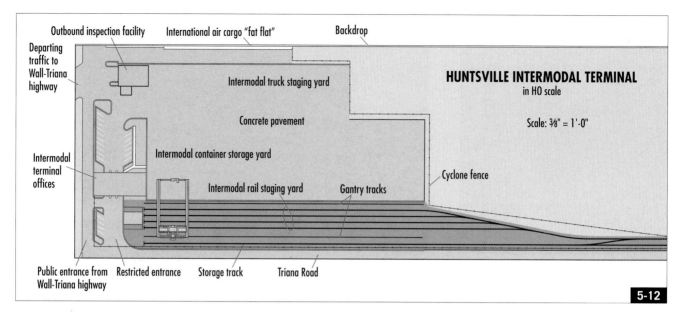

Labels on figure:
- Outbound inspection facility
- International air cargo "fat flat"
- Backdrop
- Departing traffic to Wall-Triana highway
- Intermodal truck staging yard
- Intermodal terminal offices
- Concrete pavement
- Intermodal container storage yard
- Intermodal rail staging yard
- Gantry tracks
- Cyclone fence
- Public entrance from Wall-Triana highway
- Restricted entrance
- Storage track
- Triana Road

HUNTSVILLE INTERMODAL TERMINAL
in HO scale

Scale: ⅜" = 1'-0"

5-12

▲ Jerry Moyers designed this HO scale LDE based on the intermodal terminal in Huntsville, Ala., to fit in a 5'-6" x 16' area.

The yard and engine facilities there are long gone, but they have been recreated as HO scale Layout Design Elements on the New England, Berkshire & Western.

Elkins, W. Va.

The Western Maryland's yard at Elkins, W. Va. (fig. 5-8, page 52), is a good example of a significant yard that is not overwhelming in size or complexity. The railroad's schematic drawing (fig. 5-9, page 52) shows the trackage at Elkins.

Elkins was in the heart of coal country, and the yard here served primarily as a place where loaded coal hoppers from outlying branches were gathered for the trip northeast to the main line at Knobmount Yard in Cumberland, Md.

Forest products, primarily pulpwood and wood chips, were also shipped out of the central Appalachians to paper mills such as the West Virginia Pulp & Paper mill at Luke, Md. Most eastbound freights had a few hoppers piled high with wood chips coupled directly behind the locomotives to avoid contaminating them with "whiffle dust" from the coal hoppers (fig. 5-10, page 53).

At Durbin, W. Va., the Elkins line connected end-to-end with the Chesapeake & Ohio's Greenbrier branch, which left the double-track

C&O main line near Whitcomb, W. Va. Some through freight existed, but this did not become a major bridge route for either railroad.

Elkins had a roundhouse and turntable as well as a car-repair shop. Just to the south (railroad west) of the depot and roundhouse was a through-truss bridge over the Tygarts Valley River. The depot itself was a two-story brick edifice, with the superintendent's office upstairs.

It was all uphill east of Elkins, including a formidable stretch known as Black Fork Grade, which in places reached an astounding 3.75 percent with curves up to 17 degrees. In the steam era, doubleheaded massive and potent 2-8-0s took the train out of Elkins to Montrose, where two more Consols were added as pushers.

Three more were cut in mid-train at Hendricks for the remainder of the run to Thomas. Beginning in 1953 and continuing well into the second-generation diesel era, first-generation EMD F-unit and Alco RS-3 haulers and helpers took over the daily battle with the mountain.

Elkins yard and the Western Maryland are gone, but some rail activity continues in the area. As a candidate for a modest-size coal marshalling yard LDE tucked deep into the mountains, Elkins is hard to beat.

Huntsville, Ala.

Huntsville, Ala., is the site of another excellent LDE candidate: a modern intermodal yard (fig. 5-11, page 53), which Jerry Moyers described in *Model Railroad Planning* 2000. He designed

Jim Senese looked to prototype industries and yards in the Bottoms area of Kansas City, including the Gold Medal Flour mill, as LDE candidates for his HO version of the Kansas City Terminal Ry.

5-13

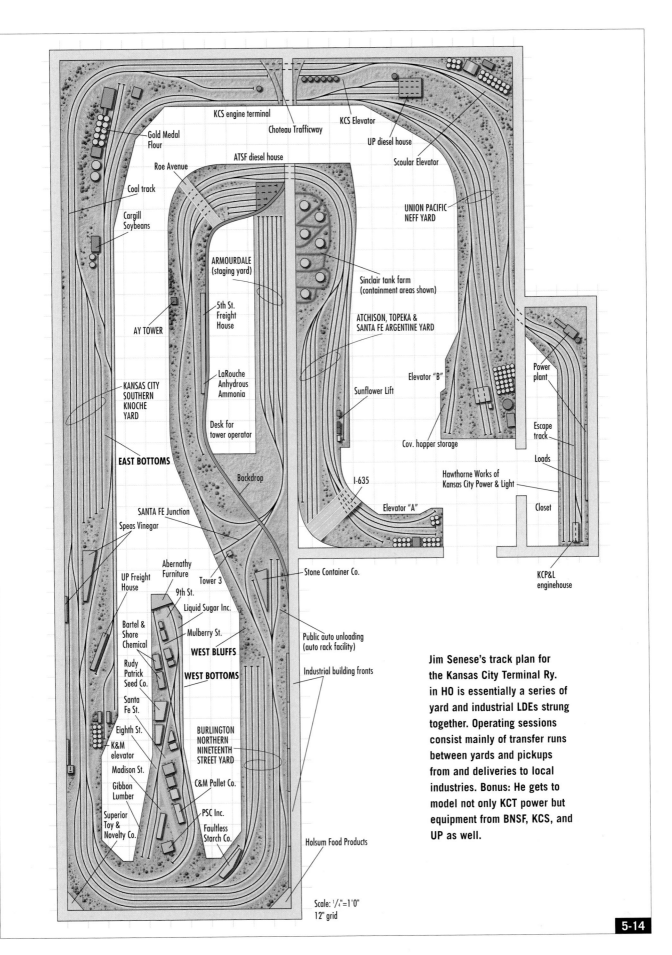

KCS engine terminal

Choteau Trafficway

KCS Elevator

Gold Medal Flour

UP diesel house

ATSF diesel house

Scoular Elevator

Roe Avenue

UNION PACIFIC NEFF YARD

Coal track

Cargill Soybeans

ARMOURDALE (staging yard)

Sinclair tank farm (containment areas shown)

AY TOWER

5th St. Freight House

ATCHISON, TOPEKA & SANTA FE ARGENTINE YARD

Power plant

KANSAS CITY SOUTHERN KNOCHE YARD

LaRouche Anhydrous Ammonia

Elevator "B"

Sunflower Lift

Escape track

Desk for tower operator

Loads

EAST BOTTOMS

Cov. hopper storage

Backdrop

I-635

Closet

Hawthorne Works of Kansas City Power & Light

SANTA FE Junction

Elevator "A"

Speas Vinegar

KCP&L enginehouse

Abernathy Furniture

UP Freight House

Tower 3

Stone Container Co.

9th St.

Liquid Sugar Inc.

Bartel & Shore Chemical

Mulberry St.

Public auto unloading (auto rack facility)

WEST BLUFFS

Rudy Patrick Seed Co.

WEST BOTTOMS

Industrial building fronts

Santa Fe St.

Eighth St.

K&M elevator

BURLINGTON NORTHERN NINETEENTH STREET YARD

Madison St.

Gibbon Lumber

C&M Pallet Co.

Superior Toy & Novelty Co.

PSC Inc.

Faultless Starch Co.

Holsum Food Products

Jim Senese's track plan for the Kansas City Terminal Ry. in HO is essentially a series of yard and industrial LDEs strung together. Operating sessions consist mainly of transfer runs between yards and pickups from and deliveries to local industries. Bonus: He gets to model not only KCT power but equipment from BNSF, KCS, and UP as well.

Scale: ¹⁄₄"=1'0"
12" grid

5-14

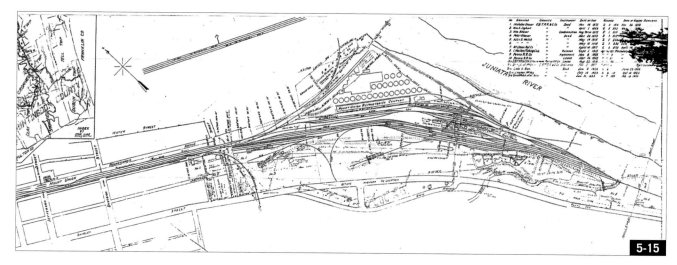

an LDE based on this terminal (fig. 5-12, page 54).

The center of attention at any intermodal terminal is the mobile crane that lifts containers on and off flatcars and truck chassis. Digital Command Control decoders and small motors have been used to control an operating wreck crane, so animating a container loading crane is feasible.

Kansas City "Bottoms"

A recent and increasingly popular trend in layout design is a large layout that features only yard and yard-transfer operations, almost to the exclusion of any mainline running at all. One trend setter in this approach to the hobby is Jim Senese. Jim lives in Oklahoma but models the industries and yards in the Kansas City East and West Bottoms area along the river (fig. 5-13, page 54).

Jim's layout (fig. 5-14, page 55 and *Model Railroad Planning* 1999)

is essentially a series of yard and industrial LDEs supported by local switching and yard transfer runs. This allows nonstop operating sessions as well as the opportunity to model a host of local railroads, including Kansas City Terminal, Burlington Northern Santa Fe, and Kansas City Southern.

Mt. Union, Pa.

As late as the mid-1950s, the Pennsylvania RR interchanged with the three-foot-gauge East Broad Top at Mt. Union, Pa., offering the opportunity to model both standard- and slim-gauge railroads on one LDE in the steam-to-diesel transition era (fig. 5-15). How that interchange was accomplished provides an interesting example for prototype modelers and freelancers alike.

▲ Mt. Union, Pa., was where the narrow-gauge East Broad Top interchanged with the Pennsylvania RR. EBT's coal prep plant was located here.

The EBT's primary product was bituminous coal. The coal was not cleaned and sized at the mines but rather was hauled out of the mountains to a large preparation plant in Mt. Union (fig. 5-16). That plant was the key to the EBT's viability for years after most Eastern slim-gauge lines had folded their tents. The coal had to be unloaded from the EBT's twin and triple hoppers for cleaning and sizing, so no extra work was required to reload it into standard-gauge hoppers for the trip to market.

Inbound loads in standard-gauge box cars, flat cars, and tank cars could have their lading transferred to narrow-gauge cars, but the EBT created a more novel solution: One of their two standard-gauge 0-6-0s switched cars from the PRR to the track that ran

The EBT brought raw coal to the preparation plant at Mt. Union, where it was dumped, cleaned, sized, and reloaded into standard-gauge hoppers for shipment to customers via the PRR (1953 photo by Philip R. Hastings). Near the prep plant was the old timber transfer crane, shown in a 1949 photo by Charles S. Small, which was used to lift one end of standard-gauge freight cars so narrow-gauge trucks could be installed.

under the timber transfer crane, where one end of a standard-gauge car could be raised and its truck rolled out of the way. Several men then rolled a narrow-gauge truck under the car, and the procedure was then repeated at the other end of the car. An aluminum knuckle casting was dropped into the regular coupler to change the height to match narrow-gauge equipment. Once the car had been retrucked, it could head south into EBT country.

In addition to coal and general freight operations, the EBT also delivered gannister rock—it looked like white coal in the hoppers!—mined below Orbisonia to brick refractories in Mt. Union. The Juniata River ran along the north side of the yard, suggesting a place to put the main access aisle.

This LDE candidate offers the chance to model not only two different railroads but both standard- and narrow-gauge lines and several interesting industries set amid verdant mountain ridges in a modest area.

Troy, N. Y.

Except for the Harrisburg LDE (fig. 5-4), the yard LDEs we've reviewed have been primary freight yards. Now let's look at a yard that served a small

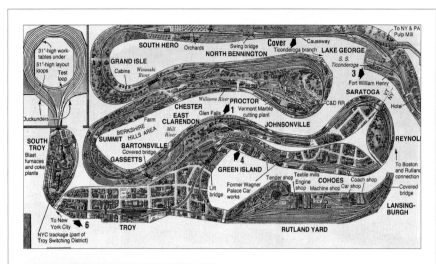

The RPI club's New England, Berkshire & Western features memorable scenes from the Northeast built as Layout Design Elements, including Troy (N. Y.) Union Station and the Rutland RR yard in the railroad's namesake city in Vermont, as shown in this photo and small section of the HO track plan.

5-17

but busy passenger station: Union Station at Troy, N. Y., which is across the Hudson River from the Empire State's capital, Albany. It served the Boston & Maine, New York Central, and Delaware & Hudson. The Rutland also came into the station via trackage rights over the B&M (see fig. 5-6).

It was once a very busy place; John Nehrich notes that in 1910 there were 130 trains per day through Troy, an average of one every 11 minutes! And almost every train had to change engines. (Popular as the steam–diesel transition era is, this suggests we ought to be looking more closely at the turn-of-the-20th-century period!)

Appropriately, the classic Union Station area is a featured Layout Design Element (fig. 5-17) on the HO scale New England, Berkshire & Western RR at nearby Rensselaer Polytechnic Institute in Troy. An unusual aspect of the station area was elevated towers that straddled both the north and south entrances to the station trackage (fig. 5-18). Imagine the sound and smoke that blasted into the confines of this catbird seat as a steam locomotive accelerated out of town!

Even if space precludes modeling a union station of such magnitude as an LDE, adding the towers to an existing yard throat—perhaps by grafting the top story of an interlocking tower kit onto a revamped signal bridge—would make a distinctive scene.

5-18

▲ This scene at the north end of the Troy, N.Y., Union Station of Rutland train 64, the southbound *Green Mountain*, was photographed by William D. Middleton in 1950. Decades later, an HO model of Union Station and its track-straddling towers highlights the New England, Berkshire & Western at RPI.

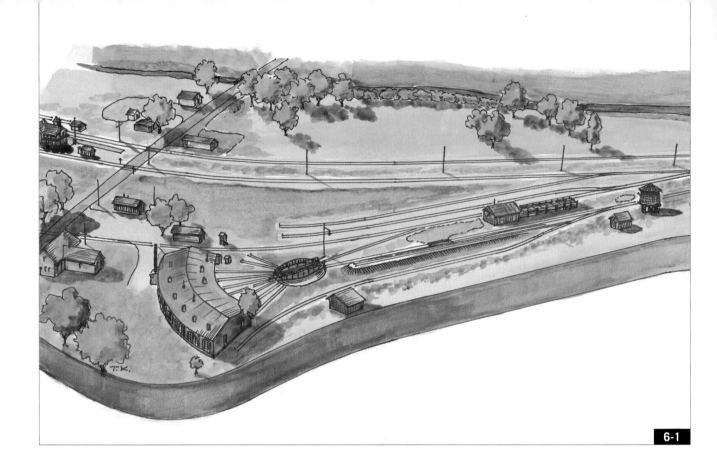

6-1

CHAPTER SIX
Engine terminals

▲ Ridgway, Colo., was located in a valley between towering mountain ranges where the north end of the Rio Grande Southern connected to another three-foot-gauge line, the Denver & Rio Grande, to form a link in the "Narrow Gauge Circle." That connection plus the small yard and engine terminal make Ridgway a promising candidate for use as a Layout Design Element. The author's sketch shows the key structures around the engine terminal.

Locomotive servicing terminals are typically combined with major yards (see Chapter 5), but they warrant a closer look as Layout Design Element candidates in this chapter. Marty McGuirk's book, *Model Railroader's Guide to Locomotive Servicing Facilities* (Kalmbach Books, 2001) provides a detailed overview of the workings of engine terminals. Like classification yards, major engine terminals range from large to huge—well beyond the scope of most modeling projects. That leaves us with three choices: switch to a much smaller scale; scale down the scope of the terminal using selective compression; or choose a small terminal to model. Let's start small.

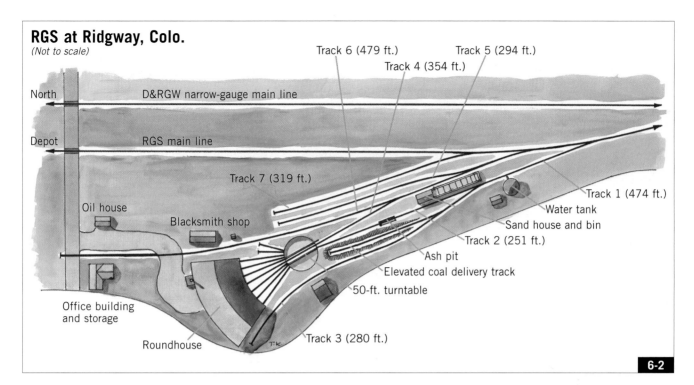

RGS at Ridgway, Colo.
(Not to scale)

North

D&RGW narrow-gauge main line

Track 6 (479 ft.)
Track 5 (294 ft.)
Track 4 (354 ft.)

Depot

RGS main line

Track 7 (319 ft.)

Track 1 (474 ft.)
Water tank
Sand house and bin

Oil house

Blacksmith shop

Track 2 (251 ft.)

Ash pit
Elevated coal delivery track

50-ft. turntable

Office building
and storage

Roundhouse

Track 3 (280 ft.)

6-2

Rio Grande at Ridgway

The Rio Grande Southern's engine terminal at Ridgway, Colo. (figs. 6-1 through 6-3, page 59) would require little or no selective compression to model accurately. In fact, I drew the plan to closely approximate the prototype's actual footprint. Even in O scale with 3" track spacing and a 6" aisle-to-track margin, the width could be held to around the 30" that is generally regarded as a maximum—except for the roundhouse area, which would have to project into the aisle. Closing up the generous spacing between the D&RGW and RGS mains and reducing the number of roundhouse stalls would reduce the overall width.

Bob Walker models the RGS in On3, and he managed to build an almost foot-for-foot copy of the Ridgway terminal area. That's not as extravagant as it may seem; measuring an RGS track drawing shows the distance from the back wall of the roundhouse to the turnout where the turntable lead joins the RGS main line to be about 650 feet. That's less than 14 feet in On3 or On2½.

Those in Sn3, HOn3, or Nn3 shouldn't be challenged for space at all. Steve Harris's HOn3 depiction of the engine terminal at Ridgway fits onto a

▲ **Ridgway is compact enough to be used without significant length compression in any scale from Nn3 to On2½ or On3. The distance from the back of the roundhouse to the engine-lead turnout off the RGS main would be under 14 feet in O scale, just over half that in HO. It would have to be compressed in width or located on a peninsula for access to both sides in the larger scales, however, as the distance from the D&RGW main to the lower corner of the roundhouse scales out to more than six feet in O.**

shelf that is under two feet wide (fig. 6-4, page 60). To make things fit better, he relocated the D&RGW-RGS depot at the turntable end of the roundhouse.

Freelancers in standard gauge could use Ridgway as a pattern without tossing plausibility into the wind. The key elements are all here: roundhouse, turntable, ash pit, sand house, water tower, and coal bin.

Ridgway offers another "triple threat" opportunity, with LDE candidates for not only the engine terminal but also a small nearby yard and a junction. This is where the RGS connected end-to-end to the Denver & Rio Grande line down from Montrose, thus forming part of Colorado's fabled Narrow Gauge Circle.

The RGS-D&RGW connection at Ridgway and the RGS's hand-me-down relationship with its parent company allows modeling the equipment of two different, if closely related, railroads. By the turn of the century, slim-gauge lines tended to exist in isolation, so this is an unusual

opportunity for prototype modelers and prototype-based freelancers alike.

Drawing the line

Before we look at several other engine terminal LDE candidates, let me raise a concern that I'll again address in chapter 7. There is a difference between modeling the essential elements of an engine terminal or any other type of LDE and blatantly copying its every nuance. The latter approach is precisely what the prototype modeler should be doing, but it presents potential perils for the freelancer.

Take South Fork, W. Va., on my former Allegheny Midland, for example. The engine terminal here was loosely based on Cane Fork (fig. 6-5, page 60), a small Chesapeake & Ohio engine terminal and yard on a coal branch in the Mountain State. My original intention was to make South Fork look very much like Cane Fork, right down to the board-and-batten enginehouse and creek that cut across the middle of the yard there.

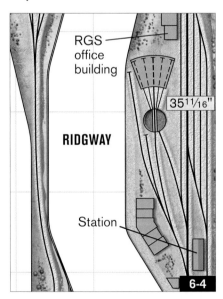

These three photos from Mallory Hope Ferrell's extensive narrow-gauge collection show the RGS's Ridgway roundhouse and nearby structures as well as a view of the water tank. Obviously, anyone modeling the RGS around 1950 will have to perfect a method of mass-producing tall weeds!

6-3

It never got to that stage; instead, I kitbashed two Walthers brick enginehouses to save time (fig. 6-6), and I never got the nerve to saw out a creek bed across the middle of the main yard to emulate the prototype.

Maybe that was good. South Fork became South Fork on the AM—and only on the AM—and Cane Fork

stayed Cane Fork on the C&O—and only on the C&O. Had I done a "better" job, knowledgeable C&O modelers might have wondered why Cane Fork was renamed and relocated.

But consider: The engine-terminal trackage arrangement in South Fork went through several revisions, and I'm not sure I ever got it "right." Perhaps I

should have copied the C&O's engine servicing track layout at Cane Fork more accurately, even if I didn't copy the structures down to the last batten.

This underscores the essence of using LDEs in a freelanced setting. We can copy the important aspects of the prototype without actually cloning it. Usually, a change of architecture is

Cane Fork, W. Va., was an outlying engine terminal for C&O Mallets and later Geeps used on mine runs. The board-and-batten enginehouse seen in an April 1954 photo by Gene Huddleston was later truncated to just the office section, as shown in Tom Dixon's October 1977 photo. The small concrete coal dock was reproduced as an HO kit by Winchester Station. Photos courtesy the C&O Historical Society.

6-5

▲ Steve Harris models the RGS in HOn3 (see the November 2004 *Model Railroader*). He has devoted one end of the lower level of his two-level layout to Ridgway. Steve relocated the depot to the south to save space.

6-4

RGS office building

35¹¹⁄₁₆"

RIDGWAY

Station

6-6

▲ The author originally intended to copy the C&O's Cane Fork engine terminal at South Fork on the Allegheny Midland, but a more generic version was actually built. An exact copy might have seemed out of place on a freelanced model railroad.

The Ma & Pa's locomotive-servicing facilities in York, Pa., included a rectangular-three-stall enginehouse and a turntable (see fig. 2-9, page 16). Stan White faithfully modeled the enginehouse and servicing facilities in HO scale.

6-7

alone enough to disguise an LDE's origins without losing the aesthetic and operational characteristics that endeared it to you in the first place.

Square "roundhouse"

We have already looked at the Maryland & Pennsylvania depot in York, Pa. (figs. 2-8 and 2-11). Several blocks southeast of the depot was a rectangular, cinder-block structure that served as a "round" house served by tracks from the turntable (fig. 6-7). As such, it fits into a much more compact space than the typical circular structure.

The York enginehouse was tucked into a small area between the Careva Machine Co. and a scrap yard. Like so many other aspects of the Ma & Pa, the York engine terminal looked for all the world like a model railroad with everything from a small yard and coal trestle to the turntable and enginehouse crammed into a tight space.

Stan White modeled York at one end of his HO edition of the Ma & Pa. He included the enginehouse and the ash pits—complete with a red bulb glowing through a pile of real ashes when a locomotive is spotted on the pit.

Reducing the footprint

An engine terminal with a large roundhouse eats up a lot of space. The prototype modeler depicting, say, the Chicago & North Western's steam-era roundhouse at Proviso near Chicago (fig. 6-8) in a scale larger than Z or N has some tough decisions to

6-8

▲ The almost complete circle formed by this Chicago & North Western roundhouse would take up a lot of space, even in N scale. The stalls on one side of the turntable could be truncated against a backdrop or by an aisle to save space.

make regarding access. He or she will either have to reach over part of the roundhouse to work in the yard or reach over part of the freight yard (visible at left in the photo) to nudge a balky locomotive. The C&NW roundhouse could be depicted by modeling only half of the building completely; the front half could be little more than the circular wall with doors.

On my former Allegheny Midland, I saved space by eliminating the turntable and roundhouse completely (see page 35, *Realistic Model Railroad Operation*). Inbound locomotives

paused at the coal dock and cinder pits, but they were never moved on into the nonexistent roundhouse, which was presumed to be somewhere out in the aisle. I couldn't turn locomotives, a non-issue with most diesels. With steam, I simply provided enough engines facing outbound on the ready track to cover the day's needs.

Freelancers have more options. They can opt to model a more compact engine facility such as the Virginian structure at Page, W. Va. (fig. 6-10, page 62), home to the railroad's coal-lugging 700-series Mallets. The large back-up lights atop the tenders and no apparent turntable suggest that these engines weren't turned at the end of the coal branches but rather ran in reverse to the main line.

The coal dock, water columns, and sand towers are all clearly visible. Not evident is the cinder pit, but rest assured there is always one in a coal-burning railroad's engine terminal.

Think "industry"

Steam engine terminals have to provide water, coal or oil, and sand for their charges. Coal-fired engines have to dump a lot of cinders after each run (fig. 6-11), which except on the smallest of short lines have to be hauled away. Often they're used as ballast on secondary trackage.

A larger terminal is going to need an inbound track that leads to the ash pit and blow-down (boiler cleaning) area and an outbound or ready track where the hostler leaves locomotives that will soon be needed on trains. Outbound engines may need to be topped off with water after road crews pick them up.

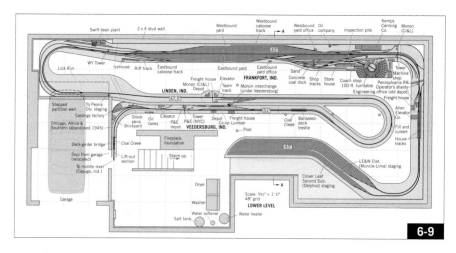

6-9

▲ The NKP engine terminal at Frankfort, Ind. (see also fig. 5-5), is a major LDE on the author's new HO layout. It is being moved several feet to the left to provide more room for the Monon crossing to its right, but the space-saving truncated stalls are being retained to maximize aisle width and reduce reach-over distance on the layout.

Cranes or hoses are needed to deliver fuel oil and water to diesels (fig. 6-12), and, like steam engines, the diesels need dry sand for spraying under their wheels to increase adhesion. As with steam, an indoor or outdoor inspection pit is needed.

In terms of operating potential on a model railroad, engine terminals therefore are essentially "industries" in that they receive large quantities of various goods (sand and coal or fuel oil plus maintenance supplies). Additionally, on most railroads east of the Rockies cinders have to be hauled away by the gondola or hopper load.

Locomotives must be able to move between the enginehouse and yard on

6-10

▲ D. Wallace Johnson photographed several 700-series 2-8-8-2s at The Virginian's engine terminal in Page, W. Va., in August 1953. Visible are most of the key ingredients of a steam locomotive's daily diet: a twin Ogle steel coal dock, sand house and towers, and a water column. Plastic Ogle coal dock kits are needed in all scales.

6-11

▲ Looking east from a platform on the NKP's concrete coal dock at Frankfort, Ind., we can see the pits where the boilers were blown down under the two 0-8-0s in the foreground and, beyond them, the two cinder pits, ash hoists, and roundhouse. The NKP car shops are off to the right in this photo from the Jay Williams (Big Four Graphics) collection.

an engine lead without forcing yard crews to wait for them to pass. The skillful design of an engine terminal is an art, which is why basing your plan on a prototype facility (see fig. 5-5) using the LDE approach is almost certain to result in a more plausible and efficient design.

Before we move on to LDEs based on signature scenes, let's consider a few more engine terminals that are potential LDE candidates.

"The Hill" at Lafayette

The Monon's main shops and engine terminal at Lafayette, Ind., were perched on a hill bordering the east side of the yard (fig. 6-13). When locomotives completed their runs, they went up to "the Hill" for servicing and inspections. The concrete coal dock, which also provided locomotives with sand for improved adhesion, and a turntable survived long after steam's demise.

The massive, multi-bay shop buildings included a transfer table. These served as prototypes for several Walthers kits, easing the chores of

The Clinchfield's modest engine-servicing facilities at Dante, Va., included a single-stall enginehouse, a sand tower fed by covered hoppers spotted nearby, and a diesel fueling area supported by a tank car next to a fuel unloading crane. For something a bit bigger, try the overhead sand bins near the CRR's two-stall enginehouse in Erwin, Tenn. (above).

6-12

modelers who want to construct a similar Layout Design Element.

The Wabash River lies just west of the yard, which suggests putting the aisle "in" the river. This creates a substantial reach over the yard to the engine servicing facilities—not ideal but probably better

than trying to stand on the east side of the shops/yard complex and trying to switch the yard over the engine terminal and shops. The fact that the engine servicing area sits high above the yard should make it easier to reach, but providing a rear access aisle might be worthwhile.

The Monon's main classification yard ran north-south along the east side of the Wabash River valley in Lafayette, Ind. (1966 black-and-white photo by Keith E. Ardinger). The Shops and engine-servicing facilities were on "the Hill."

6-13

Lloyd Keyser used this Milwaukee Road engineering drawing and several photos, including this one taken in 1939 by Ted Schnepf, to create an LDE based on the small yard and engine terminal at Wausau, Wis.

6-14

Wausau, Wis.

In the 1999 edition of *Model Railroad Planning*, Lloyd Keyser described how he worked from a Milwaukee Road blueprint to create an LDE of part of Wausau, Wis. (fig. 6-14). To ensure that accurate models of the structures near the engine terminal would fit as planned, Lloyd first made cardstock mock-ups (fig. 6-15).

Lloyd's Wausau project is a fine example of choosing a modestly sized candidate for an LDE so that it can not only be modeled accurately but also won't consume more than its share of the layout space. As Lloyd put it, "Only twice have I driven into a railroad town and felt it looked like something I would expect to see on a model railroad, but blown up to actual size. Both towns were in Wisconsin: Columbus and Wausau, the latter the hometown of the depot made famous by Wausau Insurance Co.'s advertising."

Moreover, since Lloyd's primary modeling interest is the Chicago & North Western, including a Milwaukee Road branch and engine terminal provided an opportunity to model another notable railroad in that region.

Grundy, Va.

When Bruce Meyer found the Norfolk & Western's engine terminal at Grundy, Va., deep in coal country, it was like coming upon a nest of fire-breathing dragons intertwined in a fitful sleep. The wave of dieselization engulfing less remote regions of the nation's rail network had seemingly forgotten Grundy.

In the 1950s, Grundy was home to a number of the N&W's potent 2-8-8-2

This plan shows the HO scale LDE Lloyd Keyser designed for the Milwaukee Road yard and engine terminal at Wausau, Wis. Cardstock mockups uncovered a lack of space for the water tower and a need for the coal dock to straddle one track.

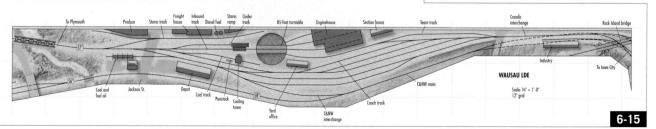

6-15

Y6b Mallets (fig. 6-16). It was indeed remote, located where the branch south from Devon, W. Va., split to reach Page and Jewell Valley. You could study a railroad atlas for a long time before you'd come up with more evocative Appalachian place names than those found on this branch.

It's easy to sense the excitement and drama photographer Meyer experienced when he encountered these machines. At this equally remote juncture in time, using Grundy as a pattern for an LDE is the only hope we have of seeing such a scene hiss and snort its way back to life.

Olean, N. Y.

Tucked neatly inside a wye on the bank of the Olean River in western New York was a compact engine terminal (fig. 6-17) that serviced steam locomotives of the Pittsburg, Shawmut & Northern RR. The PS&N's Olean branch left the main line at Prosser, N. Y., and crossed the river before entering Olean. Space was so tight that two legs of the wye were situated partially on the bridge.

The wye precluded the need for a turntable, and no enginehouse was

6-16

▲ Bruce Meyer discovered Jurassic Park in the form of the N&W's outlying engine terminal at Grundy, Va., in March 1959. By then, still-potent "dinosaurs" like these Y6b 2-8-8-2s had vanished from most other parts of the nation's rail system. Remote engine terminals like Grundy were common in the Appalachian coal fields.

provided. Coal was supplied from hoppers spotted over a pit via a conveyor to locomotives that, photos show, were backed into a depressed track. The ash pit was on the adjacent track, and I suspect they spotted a gondola at the low end of the depressed track to make it easier to shovel out the cinders. Water was provided by a between-the-track water column.

The lower-left leg of the wye went under a road bridge to reach the interchange with the Pennsylvania RR. The right leg continued into Olean to reach the depot and several breweries, which were a major source of carloadings. (Brewery production apparently continued unabated through the Prohibition Era, as the law was locally interpreted to apply only to those who belonged to the political party not in power at the time!)

Perry Squier models the Shawmut in 1923, including the wye and engine terminal at Olean. Like the prototype, it connects to breweries and the depot in Olean as well as to the PRR interchange hidden behind the backdrop. Perhaps you saw Perry and his HO railroad on the December 26, 2004, edition of Charles Osgood's *Sunday Morning* TV show on CBS.

Olean is a natural LDE candidate for PS&N modelers and could readily be adapted for use as a compact freelanced branch- or shortline terminal.

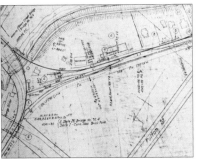

Olean, N.Y., was at the "upper-left" end of the Pittsburg, Shawmut & Northern's Y-shaped main line. Tucked neatly into a wye at the end of the bridge over Olean Creek was the PS&N's small engine terminal, as shown by this valuation map. Perry Squier, who models the Shawmut ca. 1923, built an HO scale LDE based on the PS&N's compact engine terminal inside the wye in Olean.

6-17

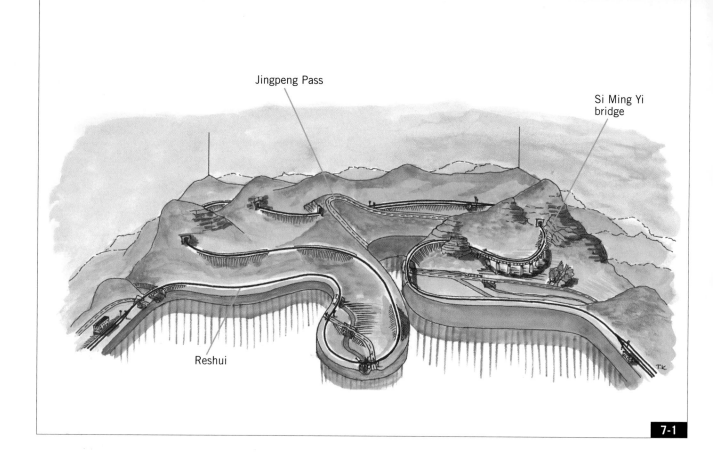

Jingpeng Pass

Si Ming Yi bridge

Reshui

CHAPTER SEVEN

Signature scenes

▲ Until recently, Jingpeng Pass in Inner Mongolia hosted numerous daily freights behind double-headed QJ 2-10-2s of USRA heritage. Its twisting climb to the summit penetrated stark ridges and leaped over high valleys on concrete bridges. Despite its foreign ancestry, China Rail's Jitong line can be used to create a scenic Layout Design Element as suggested by this sketch. The author combined four LDEs, outlined in red in fig. 7-2, with the Reshui LDE "bent" around a corner to create this plan. Use the turnback-curve diameter to gauge overall dimensions—48″ to 72″ diameter in HO, for example. On a layout, the reach-in distance to the top of the three levels at Reshui would have to be planned carefully or access from the rear must be provided.

A "signature scene" is a well-known, easily recognizable location that helps establish the identity of the railroad passing through or by it. To make the point, let's travel halfway around the world to Inner Mongolia to visit spectacular Jingpeng ("jing-pung") Pass midway on China Rail's Jitong line. This recently built line was the home to a number of CR's 3,000-hp QJ-class 2-10-2s, which had their roots in the USRA light 2-10-2—until 2005 when the line was dieselized. Jingpeng Pass has drawn railfans, the author among them, from every corner of the planet.

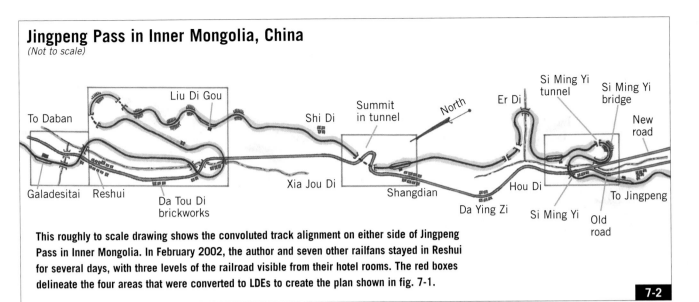

Jingpeng Pass in Inner Mongolia, China
(Not to scale)

To Daban — Galadesitai — Reshui — Da Tou Di brickworks — Liu Di Gou — Shi Di — Xia Jou Di — Summit in tunnel — North — Shangdian — Da Ying Zi — Er Di — Si Ming Yi tunnel — Si Ming Yi — Si Ming Yi bridge — Hou Di — Old road — New road — To Jingpeng

This roughly to scale drawing shows the convoluted track alignment on either side of Jingpeng Pass in Inner Mongolia. In February 2002, the author and seven other railfans stayed in Reshui for several days, with three levels of the railroad visible from their hotel rooms. The red boxes delineate the four areas that were converted to LDEs to create the plan shown in fig. 7-1.

7-2

Domesticating Jingpeng

One glance at the trackage required to get up to, over, and back down from the pass (fig. 7-2) suggests that this part of the Jitong line would make an excellent scenic LDE candidate for a freelanced model railroad on this side of the Pacific Ocean. I hope you agree after viewing my perspective sketch in fig. 7-1 and the photos in fig. 7-3.

You could take this domestication process even further by following John Swanson's example. He needed a light 2-10-2 for his HO Dixon, Wyanet & Lake Superior, a Midwestern railroad set in the 1920s, so he removed the smoke deflectors and added typical Wyanet appliances to Bachmann models of the China Rail QJ (fig. 7-4, page 68). During the first conversion, John also removed the skyline casing atop the boiler that hides the dry pipe, but he decided that was too much work for his entire fleet of QJs.

The lesson for the freelancer is that a favorite scene—maybe even a favorite locomotive—from a foreign railroad can be adapted for use on a North American railroad.

Freelancer's dilemma

Perhaps more so than with other types of LDEs, however, we need to keep in mind the "proprietary" nature of certain scenes. We all know that Horseshoe Curve (fig. 7-5, page 68) is located on the Pennsylvania Railroad (later Penn Central, then Conrail, and now Norfolk Southern) just west of Altoona, Pa. That's good or bad news, depending on your objective: Build a horseshoe-shaped, multi-track main line around a locomotive displayed in a park at the apex of the curve, and even a casual observer is bound to associate your model with the Pennsy or its successors. If that's your goal, great! If not, you've fallen into a trap.

Those of us who model a specific prototype at a given time and place make every effort to replicate actual scenes. If you're a freelancer and have bought into the Layout Design Element approach, you might reasonably conclude that copying a piece of the prototype is your best, most efficient, and risk-free option.

To some degree, the whole idea of freelancing is to express your individuality. Otherwise, why freelance? But the LDE approach suggests a little of that goes a long way when it comes time to make key decisions about a model railroad's design. That's because our knowledge of how and why a full-size railroad goes about its business may be deficient, especially at the early stages of a model railroad's

The barren landscape makes the trains look like Z scale models on Jingpeng Pass as the railroad pops out of a tunnel and begins an S curve across the valley on a spectacular concrete bridge at Si Ming Yi.

7-3

China Rail built 4,700 class QJ 2-10-2s through 1988, but they recently lost out to diesels on Jingpeng Pass. A small fleet of Bachmann's fine HO model of the QJ was given a Burlington look by John Swanson for his Dixon, Wyanet & Lake Superior. John also took the model photos.

7-4

▲ Park a locomotive at the apex of a four-track mainline curve, and it's unlikely to be identified as anything other than the Pennsylvania's world-famous Horseshoe Curve. It's now operated by Norfolk Southern, and the K4 has been replaced by a Geep.

7-5

The author measured and photographed the C&O's depot and division offices at Thurmond, W. Va., to ensure that his HO model was accurate right down to the two-tone gray paint. But he used it on his model of the AM at South Fork, not the C&O at Thurmond. Did this create a mixed and possibly confusing message to the knowledgeable viewer?

7-6

development. So the LDE approach recommends looking to the prototype for good examples to copy.

Knowing when to crib

The LDE approach can be mishandled, however. In fact, I think I came close to going down the wrong path a few times on the Allegheny Midland. I discussed concerns about my design for the engine terminal at South Fork in Chapter 6. Similar concerns arose when I scratchbuilt a model of the C&O's classic—and still standing—two-story depot and division offices at Thurmond, W. Va. (fig. 7-6). Save for the roofing (tar paper instead of shingles), it was an accurate model of the C&O structure. But, a C&O fan might wonder, why was it labeled "South Fork"? Why did the AM hijack it? And why didn't T.K. just bite the bullet and model the C&O? If it walks like a duck . . . .

In fact, all AM depots were copies of C&O structures, but most were based on a standard design that was also used by the Wabash, Missouri Pacific, and perhaps some other railroads, which made it fair game for the freelancer. Like Thurmond/South Fork, I painted them in C&O's two-tone gray scheme, but that may have been a misstep. Perhaps a more reasonable approach would have been for me to adopt a different paint scheme and apply subtle architectural details that made the structures distinctly AM. As it was, I created a source of confusion for those who, like me, admire the C&O.

Why, indeed, didn't I just model the C&O in the first place? Like many freelancers, I had modeling goals that no single prototype could satisfy. The AM therefore combined aspects of several favorite railroads, notably the scenery and structures of the C&O and, usually, the motive power and rolling stock of the NKP. It wasn't until my modeling objectives switched from hauling coal out of the Appalachians to running a high-speed bridge line across the flatlands that I found a prototype that met almost all (nothing is perfect!) of my current objectives.

The lesson for freelancers is to look

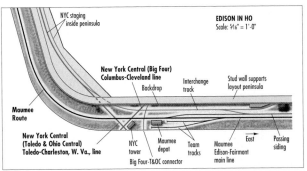

Two lines of the New York Central System crossed near the tower at Edison, Ohio. Bill Darnaby overlaid the Maumee Route main line to create a triple crossing but otherwise modeled the junction as it actually existed. (Bill Darnaby photo; Kellie Jaeger illustration) **7-7**

to the prototype for model-worthy examples of trackage arrangements. But use caution when modeling an entire scene complete with distinctive structures and scenic elements.

An exception to this premise is Bill Darnaby's depiction of Edison, Ohio, as an LDE (fig. 7-7). He modeled an actual scene where two New York Central lines crossed, then superimposed the freelanced Maumee Route's main line through the same junction. He altered reality but did not blatantly ignore or transplant it.

Town relocation

The New England, Berkshire & Western, a spectacular HO railroad designed and built by club members at Rensselaer Polytechnic Institute in upstate New York, ventured into a similar bed of quicksand as the one I encountered on the AM. The RPI modelers faithfully replicated not only distinctive depots but entire towns as LDEs. One such town was Vergennes, Vt., which had a distinctive depot with

a second-story overhang (fig. 7-8). But they called the town Inverness; they were, after all, freelancing, and the model town wasn't geographically sited where Vergennes was known to be on the former Rutland Railroad.

When I first visited the NEB&W, I was elated to see this familiar depot and scene so well modeled. "Great job on Vergennes," I told them. "Inverness," they corrected me.

Tilt! Something was wrong, or at least there was a communications breakdown on several levels.

They have since renamed the town Vergennes. It's easier to deal with a slight geographic displacement than to get everyone to think "Inverness" when they see Vergennes. Other accurately modeled towns have similarly reclaimed their proper names on the remarkable NEB&W.

What's the fuss about?

Such concerns bother some of us more than others. Many will wonder what all the fuss is about. Others will

question why the club didn't decide to model the Rutland or the D&H in the first place and thus avoid place-name confusion. In fact, some former RPI club members are doing just that in their own homes.

This is not to suggest that prototype modeling is somehow "better" than a well-thought-out freelanced railroad. While the two approaches may be somewhat different, they are equally valid in that they both offer unique challenges and rewards. The NEB&W stands as a remarkable testimonial to skillful prototype-based freelancing.

Other signature scenes

What follows are several examples of distinctive scenic features that are unalterably associated with a specific well-known railroad. As such, they are examples of LDE candidates that help establish the locale of the full-size railroad being modeled.

Other scenes in the following pages are more generic and therefore more suitable for cloning into a freelanced

The Rutland RR depot at Vergennes, Vt., had a distinctive second-story overhang (left). The RPI club faithfully modeled it on their highly regarded HO New England, Berkshire & Western (at rear of layout photo) but initially called the town "Inverness." This caused confusion; and the town is now called "Vergennes." (Model photo by Jim Boyd.) **7-8**

setting. By reflecting on such scenes and settings, the freelancer can conjure up new mythical but plausible scenic features that become signature scenes.

Several examples of freelanced mountain railroads exist that are so well done that model railroaders have come to think of them as prototypes in their own right. Consider Allen McClelland's Virginian & Ohio, Eric Brooman's HO Utah Belt (fig. 7-9) and Harry Brunk's HOn3 Union Central & Northern (fig. 1-2). Like most freelanced railroads, Eric's UB and Allen's Virginian & Ohio were not designed using LDEs as building blocks.

Harry Brunk's outstanding UC&N is a notable exception among freelanced railroads—a series of authentic LDEs that depict actual scenes and structures along the Colorado & Southern in Clear Creek Canyon. Harry documented his quest for authenticity in *Model Railroad Planning 2002* and in the "Up Clear Creek on the Narrow Gauge" series of articles in the *Narrow Gauge & Short Line Gazette*. (Most of this extensive and highly informative series was reprinted as a softcover book of the same name.)

Despite the fact that the other freelanced mountain railroad builders cited here did not use the LDE approach, those railroads are highly regarded for both scenery and operation. Their experienced designers obviously knew what they were doing and followed the typical design practices of full-sized railroads.

For the vast majority of modelers who have less experience or lack knowledgeable friends, however, the LDE strategy provides a sound foundation for progress if their knowledge lags behind their ambitions.

A context, not an end

When building a mountain railroad, it's all too easy to create a layout that focuses too much on spectacular scenery and has too little "work" to do, such as industries and interchanges to switch. Once the scenery is complete, the railroad often lies dormant or is torn up to make way for a new scenic project. I addressed this concern in my earlier books, *Realistic Model Railroad Operation*

▲ Now in its second incarnation in a new home, Eric Brooman's Utah Belt is a freelanced railroad that has achieved virtual-prototype status among model railroaders due to its solid design and spectacular scenery reflecting the Rocky Mountain terrain it theoretically serves. Eric is an art teacher, and his skill has created the expectation that a visitor to Utah could actually see a UB westbound starting the climb toward the continental divide as it enters the San Pedro River canyon. (Eric Brooman photo)

▲ This photo by Tim Zukas of the Rio Grande Zephyr climbing the face of the Front Range in August 1979 leaves no doubt that these sedimentary rocks were formed in a deep, level basin and have since been raised and tilted as the Rockies mushroomed skyward about 10 million years ago. The distinctive Front Range formations are ideal scenic LDE candidates for Moffat Road, D&RGW, or modern UP modelers.

Anyone who has ridden the *California Zephyr* or the *Rio Grande Zephyr* from Denver to Salt Lake City remembers looping around the Big Ten curves between Denver and the Front Range. This serpentine route toward Coal Creek Canyon serves to reduce the gradient. On New Year's Day 1972, Mel Patrick photographed the Rio Grande ski train as it approached the curves. Winds topping 100 mph forced the Rio Grande to spot dirt-filled hoppers on the rim of the curve (Ray Kenley photo). Artist Mike Danneman accurately modeled the curves, including the hopper wind break, as an N scale LDE. Mike also took the photo.

7-11

and *Realistic Model Railroad Design*, so I'll review it only briefly here.

Keep in mind the hard-won experience of modelers who focused on scenic grandeur, only to find that their interest in repeatedly running trains through the scenery waned in a surprisingly short time. With little or no "operation," the layouts didn't challenge their intellectual, as opposed to their artistic, sides and failed to keep them and their friends busy for hours on end running trains.

Balance is the key: It doesn't cost any more to design a railroad that supports operation, even if the primary initial goal is the scenery. But retrofitting operation onto a poorly designed railroad can be very difficult indeed.

As with a prototype, scenery is simply the context in which a model railroad goes about its business. Enjoyable as scenery is to build and look at, it's the dynamics of railroading and purposeful action that maintain one's interest over the long haul.

Same but different

If you change the details of a scene when creating an LDE for a freelanced railroad but you keep both its operational and visual "flavor" intact, you should be in good shape. A depot in your standard architecture and colors or a different

7-13

▲ Curecanti Needle, seen in this 1936 photo by William Moedinger, was once featured on the Rio Grande's herald. From 1883 until 1890, the route through Curecanti was the D&RG's main line between Denver and Salt Lake City. The line remained on the first leg of the famous Narrow Gauge Circle route, but it was eclipsed by the standard-gauge main line over Tennessee Pass, and the "Scenic Line of the World" herald was eventually retired. The tracks were removed in 1949, and the Black Canyon of the Gunnison was flooded following the construction of dams.

7-12

▲ It's not hard to understand why this rock formation on the Rio Grande's climb toward Soldier Summit in Utah is known as Castle Gate. R.H. Kindig photographed 4-6-6-4 3700 on June 28, 1939. It would make a great LDE candidate for the D&RGW modeler but is perhaps too distinctive to be relocated for use on a freelanced railroad.

7-14

7-15

▲ That the Lizard Head rock formation west of the Rio Grande Southern is aptly named is evident in this photo of a train headed north by L.C. McClure. Modeling such signature scenes helps viewers identify the region and railroad the modeler has depicted. This scene could also be used to show that a freelanced railroad has taken over the RGS, perhaps following its abandonment, or to inspire the creation of a different but equally distinct rock formation.

▲ The distinctive rock face and retaining wall identify the location in this old stereoscope photo as the Palisades on the narrow-gauge Denver, South Park, & Pacific in Colorado. Similar memorable rock formations mark the D&RGW along the Animas River canyon north of Durango, Colo, and the East Tennessee & Western North Carolina at Pardee Point in the Doe River Gorge. All would make excellent scenic LDEs or provide inspiration for other distinctive but freelanced scenes.

type of bridge or rock formation could complement your railroad's individuality without subverting the attributes of the LDE that captured your interest in the first place.

Similar to choosing towns and industries as LDE candidates, selecting scenic LDEs doesn't require you to dig deep into your bag of artistic skills and conjure up something mythical. Rather, it's almost always easier to look to a prototype for a suitable example or even to books and magazine articles. For example, Jim Kelly suggested several LDE candidates in his book,

Trackside Scenes You Can Model (Kalmbach Books 2003).

Now let's look at several scenic Layout Design Element candidates, including some surprisingly small details that are as railroad-specific as many famous scenes.

Rock stars
John Denver had it right when he sang about the "Rocky Mountain High," a mysterious effect those mountains have on visitors. When my wife Judy and I first explored western Colorado along the route of the fabled Rio Grande

Southern, we were so mesmerized by the mountains that we actually considered buying a lot near Trout Lake. Never mind that it's 10,000 feet above sea level and under snow three-quarters of the year—or that we never vacation in the same place twice. It just seemed to be the right thing to do at the time.

Back home a week later, the effect had abated before I stripped the trees off the Allegheny Midland's verdant ridges and renamed it the "Rocky Mountain Midland."

Some modelers don't get off quite

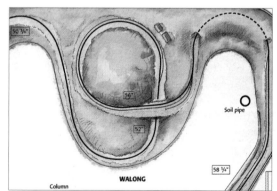

Jim Kelly has built not one but three N scale LDEs depicting the famous Tehachapi Loop at Walong, Calif., where the Santa Fe and the Southern Pacific used the extra distance around the loop to ease the grade. The photo shows version 2, and the plan shows version 3—the latter was built to be moved easily to a new home to prevent the need for a version 4.

7-16

that easily. A visit to the Rockies is enough to launch a lifelong quest to model one of the railroads that was audacious enough to push a pair of steel ribbons into, over, and through those mountains.

In so doing, we give up the advantages of a flatland railroad with crossings and interchanges with other railroads every dozen miles. We gain spectacular scenic vistas and operational challenges such as using head-end or mid-train helpers and rear-end pushers. Moreover, train speeds tend to be slower in the mountains, which also lengthens a run over the railroad.

Paying tribute to the Front Range geology by accurately modeling its tilted sedimentary rocks (fig. 7-10, page 70) is as important to the authenticity of a miniaturized Moffat Road or Rio Grande as accurately painting or superdetailing a locomotive. A scene depicting the dipping stratified rock is as much an LDE candidate as one based on a town or major industry. And slapping on rock castings this way and that isn't going to get you there.

Other Rio Grande landmarks between Denver and Salt Lake City include the Big Ten Curves (fig. 7-11, page 71) and Castle Gate (fig. 7-12, page 71). Some landmarks that took millions of years to form

7-17

▲ Williams Loop on the Western Pacific (now UP) east of Quincy, Calif., would make an interesting LDE. In September 1953, W.E. Malloy, Jr., photographed an eastbound that moments before had passed under the spot where FT 905A is now.

have very short staying power in the marketplace, however. Curecanti Needle (fig. 7-13, page 71), located deep in the Black Canyon of the Gunnison River, was once so closely associated with the Rio Grande that it was featured on the railroad's herald. (The railroad modestly described itself as the "Scenic Line of the World.") Once the Rio Grande's main line and part of the D&RG-RGS "narrow gauge circle," this narrow-gauge route was relegated to second-class status when the Tennessee Pass line

was built. Much of the old right-of-way was flooded when the river was dammed, and Curecanti Needle's status as a corporate icon sank as well.

A similar and even better-known geographic landmark is Lizard Head (fig. 7-14) near the Rio Grande Southern. Half a century after the railroad's demise, it remains a novelty for tourists. Copying such a well-known landmark for a freelanced railroad could generate a confusing message. However, creating a similar but unique landmark on a freelanced railroad in the spirit of this LDE candidate could add scenic interest and plausibility to a might-have-been railroad.

In central Colorado, the Palisades (fig. 7-15)—not to be confused with the columns of basalt of the same name that border the Hudson in New Jersey—will forever be synonymous with the spunky Denver, South Park & Pacific. Modeling this stretch of sheer rock face and the short stone retaining wall as a scenic LDE is almost a given for South Park aficionados.

So what is the freelancer who fancies the Palisades to do? One could pretend the freelanced railroad obtained trackage rights over this stretch of the DSP&P. Perhaps the mythical road took over the South Park or kept this line running after the DSP&P ceased operations.

The Canadian Pacific's world-famous Spiral Tunnels in (but not through) Mt. Ogden between Hector and Fields, B.C., were bored in 1909 to reduce the 4.4-percent grade to a still tough but more manageable 2.2 percent. They'd make a great LDE candidate for a CPR layout, but their uniqueness to the Canadian Rockies would make them questionable for LDE use on a freelanced railroad set elsewhere.

7-18

One of the most popular scenic LDEs in any scale is the remote town of Ophir, Colorado, where the Rio Grande Southern looped across the valley on a wood trestle, visited the depot and overhead tipple, and left town again on another trestle. These two photos by J. W. Maxwell were taken on May 30, 1947, while riding on a Rocky Mountain Railroad Club special. The depot area is now covered by a highway. **7-19**

Loops and tunnels

Railroad civil engineers invariably faced a struggle as they tried to avoid sharp curves and steep grades when locating a new line. The goal was to balance cuts and fills—that is, the elevation was set so that the amount of material blasted out of a cut was just enough to fill in the low spots between cuts. This avoided the expense of hauling rock to or from the site.

But sometimes it was impossible to continue directly toward a distant objective without exceeding the desired gradient. The Rio Grande's Big Ten Curves discussed at the beginning of this chapter illustrate the problem and a solution. Other examples of novel engineering solutions for easing the climb rate include the Pennsylvania's Horseshoe Curve (fig. 7-5), Southern Pacific's Tehachapi Loop (fig. 7-16,

page 72), Western Pacific's Williams Loop (fig. 7-17, page 73), and Canadian Pacific's Spiral Tunnels inside Mt. Ogden (fig. 7-18, page 73). Of these examples, only Williams Loop seems sufficiently obscure for re-use as a scenic LDE candidate on a freelanced railroad—unless the mythical line shares trackage rights with the well-known actual tenant.

Before we move on to helper grades, let's discuss one more famous scene on the Rio Grande Southern: Ophir Loop (fig. 7-19), which wasn't really a loop at all. It could be considered a town LDE candidate, but most of those who have modeled it do their best to put it into a broader context. They model not only the famous mine tipple, depot, stores, and residences (is there a single Ophir structure that hasn't been offered in kit form?) but also the wood trestles and cliffs that characterize the railroad's looping arrival and departure.

Ophir could have been little more than a wide spot along the RGS right-of-way. Instead, because of the tipple straddling the railroad and the way the RGS leaps across the valley to reach the town then arcs back out of it, Ophir became known as Ophir Loop—and an iconic scene for RGS modelers. Copying its attributes without actually modeling Ophir could similarly create a worthy LDE on a freelanced narrow- or standard-gauge layout, as we'll see in Chapter 10.

Helper grades

Since model railroad main lines are so short, we have to find creative ways to lengthen each run between the end points. Multi-level layouts are

▲ The Western Maryland's Black Fork Grade east of Elkins, W. Va., was among the most challenging of any on the continent, mainly because the WM had to move heavy coal trains to the main line at Cumberland, Md. This photo by Wm. P. Price shows a typical run with 2-8-0 helpers scattered through the train. For those including a helper-grade LDE, the time to cut in, water, and remove helpers and slow speed up the mountain help compensate for the lack of trackside industries and interchanges to switch.

an increasingly popular approach to elongate the main line and the duration of the run. Modeling a railroad that ran relatively slowly, such as a short line or branch line with small locomotives and light rail, also helps lengthen each run. Frequent stops to work local industries or interchanges with crossing railroads will also extend a train's time between terminals.

Mountain railroads typically do not have closely spaced towns and industries or interchanges with crossing railroads. Competing lines typically snaked up opposite sides of the same river valley rather than crossing at grade. Offsetting this lack of traffic generation, however, is a mountain railroad's use of helper and pusher locomotives to assist trains to the summit. It takes time to add and drop a helper or pusher, and speeds tended to be much slower than freight or passenger trains would achieve across the prairies.

Thinking of a grade as a candidate for an LDE may sound strange, but consider the big picture. Unless you create LDEs for grades, you may fail to leave sufficient space for them in the layout design process.

Prior to a recently built bypass around downtown Lafayette, Ind., the Monon and its successors ran down the middle of 5th Street for decades. Much like the WP's Oakland station, the Monon's original limestone passenger station was located on this busy street. A 1971 photo shows a westbound N&W freight easing through Elwood, Ind., in 1971 on the former NKP. (See Elwood LDE in Chapter 10.)

7-21

7-22

▲ Sometimes the little things really do make a difference. If the styling of the streamlined locomotive isn't enough of a hint as to the railroad's identity, the offset bracket atop the pole brands this 1982 photo as a scene along the Norfolk & Western.

An ultimate example of a helper grade that could serve as a candidate for a Layout Design Element was the Western Maryland's climb up the Black Fork grade out of Elkins, W. Va. (fig. 7-20). This line confronted sharp curves and staggeringly steep grades. Many of the steam locomotives assigned to the division were simultaneously employed to get a single train up the mountain. Yet the line had no physical features so distinctive and widely known that they would preclude it from being used as an LDE candidate on a freelanced railroad.

The problems railroads experience with grades aren't confined to the uphill direction. Improvements in airbrakes and dynamic braking systems have eased the task somewhat, but in the steam and early diesel eras, trains had to stop at the summit to turn up air brake retainers on a number of cars, thus holding a certain amount of pressure in the braking system. The retainers had to be turned down at the bottom of the hill to release that pent-up braking pressure.

Street running
A main line down the middle of a city street, while not rare, is nonetheless unusual enough to warrant consideration as an LDE. Examples abound from

coast to coast; even the *California Zephyr* had to negotiate a length of street trackage on its way into Oakland, Calif., on the Western Pacific.

Midwestern examples include the Monon's trek down the center of the streets of several Hoosier towns including Fifth Street in Lafayette, Ind., and the Nickel Plate Road's street running through Elwood, Ind. (fig. 7-21). The slow pace forced by safety considerations during street running works to our advantage as we try to stretch our main lines by slowing trains. A section of track buried in the pavement therefore makes an excellent LDE candidate.

It's the little things
Signature scenes can be created or greatly enhanced with what may seem to be rather subtle details. All it takes is a visual trigger that leads the viewer to understand at a glance what he or she is looking at.

A good example is the offset bracket that the Norfolk & Western used atop their communication-line poles (fig. 7-22). They bespoke the line's ownership just as clearly as the N&W's use of color position light signals. The bracket itself isn't an LDE candidate, but a row of lineside poles featuring such brackets would be.

8-1

CHAPTER EIGHT

Bridges

Comparing Lou Sassi's model photo to the author's 1973 prototype photo (fig. 8-2) of the Erie's famous Starrucca Viaduct in northeastern Pennsylvania shows how accurately its "texture" was captured by Harry McGowan's model. Harry built this magnificent bridge for Harold Werthwein's HO layout, and Jim Kubanick painted and weathered it.

Bridges have long been among modelers' most favored railroad structures. They offer tremendous visual intrigue in their own right, and they span undulations in the terrain or bodies of water that themselves add scenic appeal to a model railroad. Moreover, they come in a wide variety of shapes and sizes, literally one for every occasion. Choosing suitable bridge Layout Design Element candidates is therefore less a matter of options and more a matter of deciding which ones are appropriate for the era and type of railroad being modeled and can be fit into the available space.

Railroad focal point

Illustrating the potential importance of a bridge LDE is Starrucca Viaduct (figs. 8-1 and 8-2) on Harold Werthwein's well-executed HO scale depiction of the Erie RR's Delaware Division between Port Jervis and Binghamton, N.Y. There was no need for me to sketch it; Lou Sassi's spectacular photo and a section of Harold's sprawling track plan (fig. 8-3) show it perfectly.

Think of the Erie and you can't help but picture this towering stone edifice, which is actually located at Lanesboro, Pa. When Harold made plans to model the Delaware Division, one of his major challenges was to do justice to the imposing and well-known prototype.

The model, built by Harry McGowan using individual styrene "stones" over a styrene shell, matches the prototype's height and gradient across the top, but Harry omitted six of the 18 arches to reduce its length. The bridge is still so large and impressive that viewers seldom notice the missing arches. Jim Kubanick then painted it to match the prototype.

The resulting bridge LDE is a testimonial to the skills of these modelers, to the Erie Railroad, and to the contribution that such a model can make to the appearance of the railroad.

Bridge LDE candidates

The huge variety of bridge types and sizes means that there is almost certain to be a suitable prototype for the freelancer as well as prototype modeler to use as a benchmark when planning

▲ The Starrucca Viaduct spans a creek and a branch of the Delaware & Hudson at Lanesboro, Pa. The D&H line has been abandoned, but the bridge still supports rail traffic in the 21st century. When the author photographed it, a pair of Erie Lackawanna F7s were headed back down the mountain to assist another train up to Gulf Summit.

a Bridge LDE. Moreover, since bridge engineering is somewhat of an art form where strength is paramount but aesthetics sometimes plays a major role, it's probably best to leave the technical work to the professionals and simply copy their designs.

Keep in mind that all bridges are not created equal; even the pros don't always agree on which is the best approach to a given problem. This disparity of opinion has resulted in numerous types of truss bridges, for example, each bearing the name of its developer: Warren (fig. 8-4), Pratt, and Howe, to name a few popular types.

Engineers in each railroad's bridge and building department held equally strong views about which designs best suited their needs. One therefore tends to find numerous examples of a few bridge types rather than some of these and some of those along a specific line. A railroad that grew by combining with other railroads, however, may have a variety of bridge types dating to before the mergers. Bridge replacement programs also expand bridge types.

In a few cases, bridges go a long way toward establishing the identity of a railroad. The Chicago & North Western's extensive use of the

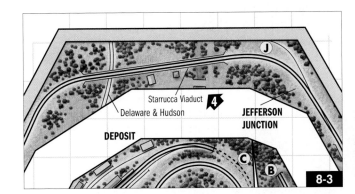

▲ The Starrucca Viaduct LDE, located in an alcove of Harold Werthwein's basement, includes a short dummy section of the Delaware & Hudson below the Erie's double-track main. As on the full-sized Erie, the viaduct forms a signature scene on the layout.

▲ One of the most common types of truss bridge is the Warren truss, identified by the W-shape of its diagonals. Shown here is a four-span Warren truss over the Wabash River on the NKP's St. Louis Division. Other common truss types include Pratt (diagonals "lean" toward the ends) and Howe (with diagonals leaning toward the center).

distinctive and intricate lattice truss (fig. 8-5), for example, ensures that any such Bridge LDE will be readily identified with the C&NW.

Before moving on to another type of LDE where rails and water come together in chapter 9, let's look at several other Bridge LDE candidates.

Speers Ferry, Va.

The Clinchfield's towering steel deck-girder trestle at Speers Ferry, Va. (fig. 8-6), is another good LDE candidate. It could be readily modeled using Micro Engineering bridge components. As with Starrucca Viaduct, N scalers could build it close to scale size, but few of us could afford the space it would take in HO or larger scales.

We can visualize this scene as having only one railroad rather than two (that's a Southern branch in the valley below the CRR), with both lines joined together behind the ridge in the background. This scene would be an appropriate LDE candidate to employ at the open end of a peninsula, thus keeping the scene visually intact despite the "merger."

8-5

Christie Studio

▲ The Chicago & North Western alone favored the lattice truss, which was used extensively all over the system. This example spanned the East Channel at Clinton, Iowa.

Feather River Canyon

Western Pacific (or, today, Union Pacific) modelers rightfully include such famous scenic features as the wye-shaped deck-girder bridges at Keddie (fig. 8-7). Another signature bridge scene on the WP in the Feather River Canyon is the arched-top-chord span bracketed by a pair of short through-truss bridges at Pulga, Calif. (fig. 8-8). It would translate well to an LDE of manageable size.

These bridges point out another small but significant characteristic that

The Clinchfield's Speers Ferry, Va., viaduct towers high above a Southern line in the river valley. An authentic-looking LDE could connect the CRR and SR lines behind the distant ridge to create a continuous single-line run around the open end of a peninsula.

8-6

Following a meet, four Western Pacific EMD FTs move a westbound freight out of the small yard at Keddie, Calif., and onto the Keddie Wye bridge. The line to the left uses the Inside Gateway through Bieber, Calif., to reach connections in Oregon. Keddie has long been a popular LDE candidate for WP modelers or for those modeling this part of what is now the Union Pacific. Western Pacific photos

8-7

helps reinforce a railroad's identity: paint. Just as some railroads painted signal masts black while others painted them aluminum, railroads painted their bridges in hues ranging from sedate black to gleaming silver or even pale green.

Glen Lyn, Va.

The Virginian's bridge over the Narrows section of the New River at Glen Lyn, Va. (fig. 8-9) is another signature structure. Like Speers Ferry and Starrucca Viaduct, it offers the prototype modeler a chance to build parts of two railroads, as the Norfolk & Western passed underneath its western end. A freelancer could combine the two lines by connecting them off to the west, which is exactly what happened following the 1959 merger of the Virginian into the N&W. (Unfortunately, this eventually led to the demolition of the bridge.)

Stoney Creek, B. C.

The distinctive construction and international fame of the Canadian Pacific's steel-arch Stoney Creek viaduct (fig. 8-10) in British Columbia's Glacier Park makes it a questionable candidate for a freelanced railroad, but it would certainly help to set the scene for a CPR layout. Some years ago at an NMRA national convention, I saw an HO model of this bridge and, as you might expect, it attracted quite a crowd.

8-8

▲ Motorists driving along the Feather River on Hwy. 70 can't miss this view of the Western Pacific (Union Pacific) truss bridges at East Pulga, Calif., where Extra 3530 West was photographed by Donald R. Kaplan on June 22, 1981.

8-9

▲ Virginian Extra 103 East heads over the New River Narrows bridge at Glyn Lyn, Va., trailing coal and general freight. As at Speers Ferry (fig. 8-6), the VGN could loop around the ridge to the west and reappear as the N&W line past the power plant at left. Richard J. Cook photo

8-10

▲ CP Rail Extra 5835 East crosses the famous Stoney Creek viaduct on its descent from the summit in British Columbia's Glacier Park in June 1975. Steve Patterson photo

8-11

▲ Among the many examples of covered wood bridges on the Boston & Maine was this one at Bennington, N.H. The center pier may have been added to strengthen the old bridge, which Glenn A. Wagner photographed in June 1947. Such bridges might look out of place in other regions, but they help to identify this railroad's Granite State setting.

8-12

8-13

▲ The twin-span covered bridge near Claremont, N.H., on the B&M was later used by the shortline Claremont & Concord. The Don Valentine photo evident in the foreground inspired this scene on a No. 1 scale project railroad the author built for *Model Railroader*. A mirror makes the single span appear to be a double-span bridge.

▲ Concrete arch bridges are among the most durable of railroad structures, and they can be formed to smoothly accommodate curves. The author photographed this eastbound coal train trailing brake-shoe smoke on the double-track B&O (Chessie System) main line at Luke, Md., in May 1976.

Chandler, N. H.

A primary reason to model one of the Boston & Maine's scenic branch lines in New Hampshire is the opportunity to include one of its famous covered bridges. Some were just a single span (fig. 8-11, page 79), but others, including the bridge over the Sugar River just east of Claremont, N. H., at Chandler were longer. I used a mirror to double the apparent length of a No. 1 scale (⅜" to the foot) factory-assembled model of the latter bridge (fig. 8-12) on a project railroad I built for *Model Railroader* magazine, a trick that works especially well with a covered bridge in that it hides the hole in the mirror.

Luke, Md.

From the outset, the Baltimore & Ohio seemed to be built for the ages. Massive masonry arch bridges were built where railroads of lesser ambitions might have used wood trestles.

A more modern example of the B&O's quest for permanence is the concrete arch at Luke, Md. (fig. 8-13). Evidence of the terrain confronting B&O planners and civil engineers is evident in the wisps of blue brake smoke emanating from the loaded coal hoppers trailing the second-generation EMD hood units.

Concrete-arch bridges weren't rare; even the three-foot-gauge East Broad Top had one at Aughwick Mills, Pa., which survives to this day, a half-century after the line ceased common-carrier operations. The Lackawanna was probably the all-time champ in concrete-arch bridge construction with spectacular examples in New Jersey and Pennsylvania. They are therefore good LDE candidates for both prototype modelers and freelancers, but their high cost of construction calls for care when choosing an application.

Sharon, Md.

Sometimes a photo has as much to do with a scene becoming famous as what's depicted in that image. Such is the case for an otherwise unremarkable wood trestle on the Maryland & Pennsylvania at Sharon, Md. James Gallagher's late-day silhouette of 2-8-0 no. 43, a solitary boxcar, and a four-wheel bobber (fig. 8-14) ranks among the all-time classic rail photographs.

Stan White modeled a similar scene on his HO Ma & Pa, but it took a bit of photographic trickery—I slid a piece of cardstock behind the trestle to get a plain background and put light only on the "sky"—to recreate the mood of Gallagher's photo.

A model photo can go a long way toward "coloring" a viewer's perception of a specific LDE and, indeed, of an entire model railroad. Smoke, sunsets, and other difficult-to-model effects may be inserted for a special photo or

James P. Gallagher's classic silhouette of Ma & Pa 2-8-0 No. 43 on a southbound one-car train at Sharon, Md., looks like a shot staged on a model railroad—which is what the author did on Stan White's HO edition of the Ma & Pa. Stan has since dismantled this porch-size layout and is planning a larger version in his new home.

8-14

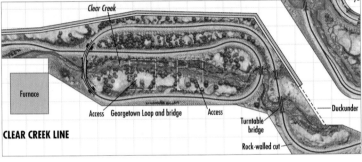

CLEAR CREEK LINE

Labels on diagram: Clear Creek, Furnace, Access, Georgetown Loop and bridge, Access, Turntable bridge, Rock-walled cut, Duckunder

Only the railroad's name is freelanced on Harry Brunk's authentic HOn3 depiction of the Colorado & Southern's Clear Creek line, which includes the famous Georgetown Loop bridge that now hosts tourist trains. The loop LDE is located in a wide spot in the benchwork in the 12' x 65' mobile home ("Little Colorado") that houses the UC&N. R.H. Kindig took the prototype photo in 1938; Harry took the model photo.

8-15

created digitally on a computer, and the resulting image can be published or hung in a place of honor in the railroad room to help viewers see the railroad in a much larger context than the actual modeling permits.

Georgetown Loop, Colo.

Build a spindly bridge high above a roaring brook and they will come—to see it and ride over it. That's what happened at the bridge that forms part of the Georgetown Loop not once but twice: when it was first built as part of the Colorado & Southern's

line up Clear Creek Canyon west of Denver (fig. 8-15), and again decades later when the dismantled bridge was resurrected as part of a tourist line between Silver Plume and Georgetown.

Harry Brunk features the creek, looping main line, and bridge as an LDE on his HOn3 depiction of this line, which he calls the Union Central & Northern. Despite the freelanced name, the railroad provides an excellent example of how to design a layout by connecting actual towns and scenes (LDEs) in the proper geographical order.

"Advertising"

Even bridges that are not widely recognized as signature structures can set the scene when they are lettered for the owning railroad (fig. 8-16).

To reinforce the idea that my freelanced Allegheny Midland had trackage rights over the Western Maryland, I lettered a through-girder bridge for the WM. It has no specific prototype and hence is not a true LDE, but it underscores the point about helping viewers understand what they're seeing, especially on a freelanced railroad.

An easy way to convert an otherwise ordinary bridge scene into something more memorable, and thus a bridge LDE candidate, is to paint the railroad's name or herald on the side. The Virginian did that at Oakvale, W. Va. (Richard J. Cook photo, September 1953), as did the more modest bridge bearing the name of the Durham & Southern photographed by the author in 1973.

8-16

9-1

Railroading with a nautical flavor

▲ Matt Kosic took this aerial view of the yard and port LDE built by Arnt Gerritsen that accurately depicts the Ann Arbor facilities at Frankfort, Mich. Arnt adjusted the height of the coal dock and sand dunes to compensate for the required horizontal compression of the overall scene.

The last Layout Design Element category we'll examine is the rail-served port. Let's start with a look at Frankfort, Mich., where the Ann Arbor Railroad employed its fleet of car ferries to move freight cars back and forth across Lake Michigan. We'll then review other car ferry operations on that lake, as well as several other interesting inland car-float operations, and we'll briefly visit both ends of the shipping of iron ore and coal across the Great Lakes. Our attention will then shift to "tidewater" ports where the railroads shook hands with ocean-going ships. Finally, we'll examine a place where a little-known narrow-gauge common carrier negotiated a switchback down an embankment to meet river boats.

► This spectacular Frankfort harbor scene greets visitors descending the stairs into Arnt Gerritsen's basement. Part of the water was made removable to allow access for maintenance and photography. The entire HO railroad is a series of AA LDEs, which made it easy to run the railroad in a prototypical manner as Arnt's interest in operation blossomed.

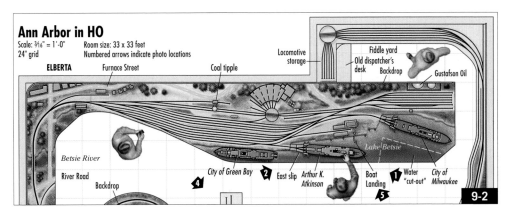

Ann Arbor in HO
Scale: ³⁄₁₆" = 1'-0"   Room size: 33 x 33 feet
24" grid   Numbered arrows indicate photo locations

ELBERTA   Furnace Street   Coal tipple   Locomotive storage   Fiddle yard   Old dispatcher's desk   Backdrop   Gustafson Oil

Betsie River
River Road   Backdrop
City of Green Bay 2   East slip   Arthur K. Atkinson   Boat Landing 5   Water "cut-out" 1   City of Milwaukee   Lake Betsie   4

9-2

9-3

▲ Arnt Gerritsen's photo of an Ann Arbor car ferry being switched at Frankfort in 1981 (left) and Matt Kosic's photo of Arnt's LDE of the same scene show where the inspiration came from and how it was creatively applied. Note that the HO version of the Annie also uses idler flats to keep the locomotive's weight off the apron.

► The Pere Marquette (later C&O, then Chessie) sent cars across Lake Michigan in car ferries that were very similar to the AA ferries. This photo from the Ted Schnepf collection shows boat 41, the *City of Midland*, being switched at Ludington, Mich.

9-4

Car floats and ferries

The opportunity to model both railroading and shipping is hard to resist. Prototype examples abound for the designer of a Layout Design Element based on a port. Long before Arnt Gerritsen had heard of the term, he instinctively used LDEs to plan his HO layout based on the Ann Arbor RR. When Arnt later became interested in prototypical operation, the railroad was ready and waiting, thanks to its prototype-based trackage arrangements.

One of the LDEs Arnt created for his railroad was the harbor scene at Frankfort, Mich. (figs. 9-1, 9-2 and 9-3). He not only modeled the nearby yard and associated apron trackage but several of the Annie's huge car ferries as well, with removable superstructures for access to the tracks inside.

The choice of a port served by car ferries is a natural choice for an Ann Arbor modeler, but it was a wise tactical decision as well. Large as those Lake Michigan car ferries may seem, they are compact compared to the

space required for a hidden staging or fiddle yard where cars can be moved on or off the visible portion of the railroad. By "sailing" the ferry, either physically by rolling it away on a cart or symbolically by removing the cars from its tracks by hand and swapping them for other cars stored in nearby drawers, the function of a passive staging or active fiddle yard is accommodated in a minimum space.

A testimonial to the wisdom of using the LDE approach to layout design was provided when a man who

83

had worked in that yard visited Arnt and observed that it was hard to switch the scale track. Arnt thought he had made a serious design error until the visitor quickly assured him that the prototype scale track had been equally difficult to switch!

The Pere Marquette, later Chesapeake & Ohio and Chessie System, also used ship-like car ferry "boats" out of Ludington, Mich., to cross Lake Michigan (fig. 9-4, page 83).

The other side

On the Wisconsin side of Lake Michigan, Ann Arbor and Pere Marquette (C&O) car ferries docked at several ports, including Kewaunee (fig. 9-5) where they were met by the Green Bay & Western. All of these would make excellent LDE candidates for the prototype modeler, and the fact that there were quite a few ports on the west side of the lake—Kewaunee, Manitowoc, Menominee, and

Milwaukee, Wis., as well as Manistique on Michigan's Upper Peninsula— means that adding a new port for a freelanced railroad wouldn't seem out of line.

Embarrassment of riches

There are myriad intriguing sites where railroads and water-borne entities worked hand in hand to transport, load, or unload carloads of freight. This vastness of opportunities means that I

▲ The AA's *Viking* is listing because freight cars on the starboard track have created a temporary imbalance. Stan Mailer photographed the ferry at Kewaunee on July 5, 1974.

▲ This late-1940's C&O photograph shows two of the railroad's three coal dumpers at Presque Isle near Toledo, Ohio.

▲ In 1950, the Nickel Plate purchased giant electric Hulett unloaders— the last ever built—to replace steam-powered Huletts bought by predecessor Wheeling & Lake Erie in 1913 to unload iron ore at Huron, Ohio. One of the new machines is shown unloading the *Saskadoc* in 1955; their careers ended in December 1985. A coal dumper was located on the east side of the next slip to the right. Photo courtesy Eric Hirsimaki (Mileposts Publishing).

▲ This company photo shows the Chicago & North Western's lengthy ore docks at Escanaba, Mich., just one of several such docks at the west end of Lake Superior that fed steel mills that rimmed the Great Lakes to the east. Walthers makes an HO kit that should simplify the construction of an LDE based on one of these huge structures that easily dwarfs a sizable lake boat. Just make sure that car-to-car spacing matches the distance between the ore pockets.

9-9

9-10

▲ The tug *Iris G* warps a barge transporting CP Rail GP9 8820 and part of its train into the slip at Rosebery, B.C., following its trip up Slocan Lake from Slocan City on September 12, 1978. The cars on the apron came up the day before and were winched ashore. They'll join the Geep, caboose, and newly arrived cars for the trip west over the Kaslo Subdivision to Nakusp. Barging was the only way cars could get to and from this isolated forest-products branch. John C. Illman photo

▲ Car ferries ranged from featureless barges moved by tug boats to self-powered, ship-like vessels. In between were the self-powered ferries with open decks and usually an elevated navigation bridge like this C&O ferry on the Detroit River. Elmer Treloar photographed the *Pere Marquette 10* on June 27, 1953.

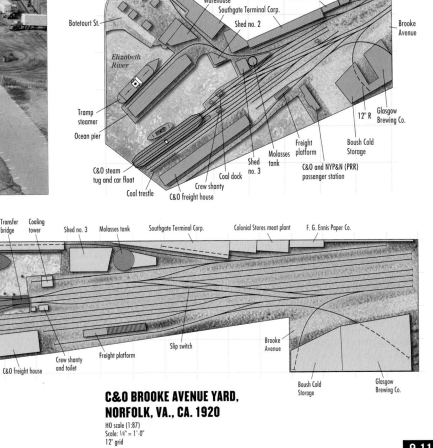

C&O BROOKE AVENUE YARD, NORFOLK, VA., CA. 1950

N scale (1:160)
Scale: ½" = 1'-0"
12" grid

Thomas St. — Access — F. G. Ennis Paper Co. — Colonial Meats — Warehouse — Southgate Terminal Corp. — Botetourt St. — Shed no. 2 — Brooke Avenue — Elizabeth River — 12" R — Glasgow Brewing Co. — Tramp steamer — Ocean pier — Freight platform — Boush Cold Storage — Molasses tank — C&O steam tug and car float — Shed no. 3 — C&O and NYP&N (PRR) passenger station — Coal dock — Crew shanty — C&O freight house — Coal trestle

Bernie Kempinski found an ideal prototype for a nautical-theme LDE in the C&O's Brook Avenue Yard in Norfolk, Va. This photo from the C&O Historical Society's collection looks west toward the Elizabeth River in 1956. Bernie designed both N and HO scale LDEs based on this compact scene.

Tramp steamer — Ocean pier — Transfer bridge — Coaling tower — Shed no. 3 — Molasses tank — Southgate Terminal Corp. — Colonial Stores meat plant — F. G. Ennis Paper Co. — Slip switch — Brooke Avenue — Car float and tugboat — C&O freight house — Crew shanty and toilet — Freight platform — Boush Cold Storage — Glasgow Brewing Co.

C&O BROOKE AVENUE YARD, NORFOLK, VA., CA. 1920

HO scale (1:87)
Scale: ¼" = 1'-0"
12" grid

9-11

can offer little more than a few hints about the potential of nautical-theme LDE candidates here. I'll touch on some examples from several different categories that caught my eye, thus shining a narrow beam of light on a modeling theme that merits vastly greater study.

This review of port-based LDE candidates concludes my overview of the concepts that underlie the use of Layout Design Elements to design a prototype-based or freelanced model railroad. After we examine a few more nautical-theme LDE candidates, it will

then be time to put what we've learned into practice by using LDE "puzzle pieces" and a "game board" to design a pair of bedroom-size model railroads.

Where the coal went

All that coal hauled out of the mountains had to go somewhere, and in many cases part of its journey was to the Great Lakes and then by lake boat to steel mills and power plants. This required huge unloading structures along the southern shores of the Great Lakes such as on the Chesapeake & Ohio at Toledo (fig. 9-6, page 84)

and at Huron, Ohio, on the Nickel Plate Road (former Wheeling & Lake Erie, fig. 9-7, page 84). Many of these ports served a dual purpose, as lake boats brought iron ore in from Lake Superior ports, including Duluth, Minn., and Superior and Escanaba, Mich. (fig. 9-8, page 84), and took back loads of coal.

Canada's Slocan Lake

Far inland from the oceans or major rivers is Slocan Lake. Here, the Canadian Pacific operated a car-float operation between Slocan City and Rosebery, B. C. The "cargo" often included not only the freight cars but a locomotive and caboose, as can be seen in fig. 9-9 (page 85).

An interesting part of this operation was that the diesel didn't sail on every trip; it stayed "ashore" from Tuesday to Thursday to work the Kaslo Subdivision between Rosebery and Nakusp while the tugboat *Iris G* took the barge and previously loaded cars back down the lake to Slocan City. On Thursday, the diesel would load itself onto the barge for the trip back to Slocan City and Nelson.

A movable barge could serve as a mobile staging or fiddle yard that is

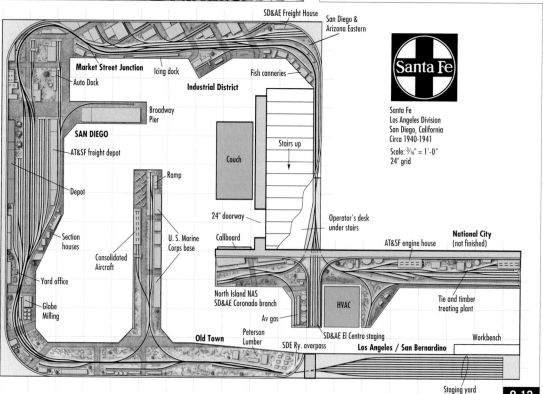

Keith Jordan planned an HO layout as a series of industrial LDEs replicating the Santa Fe tracks, piers, and industries in pre-WWII San Diego. This 1940 view looks toward the 11th District Naval headquarters above a PBY Catalina flying over the Santa Fe yards and the Padre's Lane Field.

SD&AE Freight House
San Diego & Arizona Eastern
Market Street Junction
Icing dock
Fish canneries
Auto Dock
Industrial District
Broadway Pier
SAN DIEGO
AT&SF freight depot
Couch
Stairs up
Depot
Ramp
24" doorway
Operator's desk under stairs
Section houses
U. S. Marine Corps base
Callboard
AT&SF engine house
National City (not finished)
Consolidated Aircraft
Yard office
Tie and timber treating plant
Globe Milling
North Island NAS SD&AE Coronado branch
Av gas
HVAC
Old Town
Peterson Lumber
SDE Ry. overpass
SD&AE El Centro staging
Workbench
Los Angeles / San Bernardino
Staging yard

Santa Fe
Santa Fe
Los Angeles Division
San Diego, California
Circa 1940-1941
Scale: 3/16" = 1'-0"
24" grid

9-12

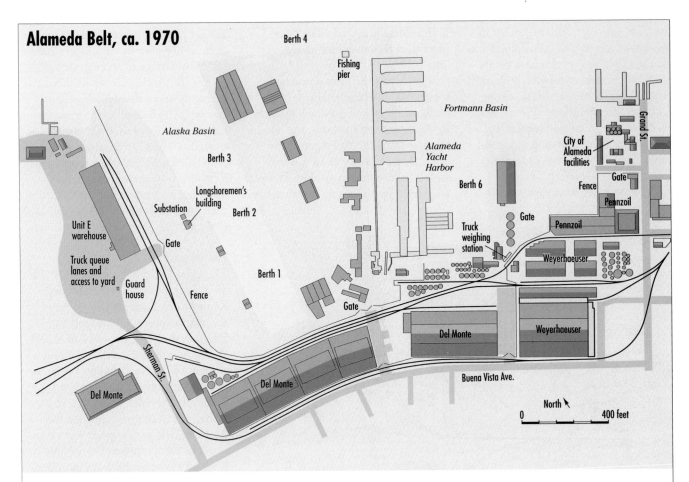

Alameda Belt, ca. 1970

Berth 4

Fishing pier

Fortmann Basin

Alaska Basin

Berth 3

Alameda Yacht Harbor

City of Alameda facilities

Longshoremen's building

Berth 6

Fence

Gate

Substation

Berth 2

Pennzoil

Unit E warehouse

Gate

Truck weighing station

Gate

Pennzoil

Weyerhaeuser

Truck queue lanes and access to yard

Guard house

Fence

Berth 1

Gate

Del Monte

Weyerhaeuser

Sherman St.

Del Monte

Del Monte

Buena Vista Ave.

North

0   400 feet

Grand St.

The Alameda Belt Line served several major industries on its namesake island in San Francisco Bay. Richard Steinheimer photographed its first Alco switcher in 1955. Byron Henderson's track plan is designed to fold for storage atop a small bookcase, but a more extensive plan could keep several operators busy for hours.

rolled or carried to a storage rack. The cars could be switched by hand between the barge and storage racks, or another barge with "yesterday's" cars could be ready to move into position.

River ferry operations

The difficulty of crossing major rivers, especially in railroading's formative years, led to a considerable number of car ferries. Some were moved by tug boats, as at Slocan Lake, B. C., while others were self-powered. The Chesapeake & Ohio's car ferry *Pere Marquette 10* (fig. 9-10, page 87) that sailed between Detroit and Windsor, Ont., is an example of the latter. As at Rosebery, the car ferry makes a convenient device to move cars on and off the railroad.

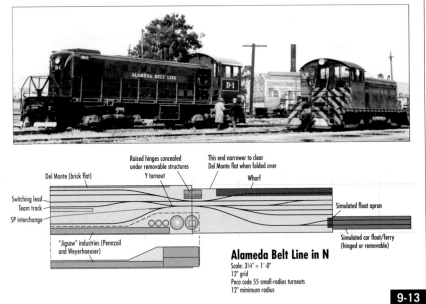

Del Monte (brick flat)

Raised hinges concealed under removable structures

Y turnout

This end narrower to clear Del Monte flat when folded over

Wharf

Switching lead
Team track
SP interchange

Simulated float apron

Simulated car float/ferry (hinged or removable)

"Jigsaw" industries (Pennzoil and Weyerhaeuser)

Alameda Belt Line in N
Scale: 3¼" = 1'-0"
12" grid
Peco code 55 small-radius turnouts
12" minimum radius

9-13

Bernie Kempinski documented another C&O cross-river car float operation as a pair of LDEs, one N scale and one HO scale. This example worked out of the small Brooke Avenue Yard in Norfolk, Va. (fig. 9-11, page 85), and utilized a tug to move the float. Its compact size, even in a

larger scale, and appealing features make it an ideal LDE.

Coal to tidewater

Coal moving from the Appalachian bituminous fields toward the Great Lakes was often called "lake" coal. Coal that moved to ocean ports was similarly dubbed "tide" coal. Although most of those who model coal railroading focus on the tipples and preparation plants at the origination end of the cycle, port facilities offer considerable modeling and operational rewards of their own.

An ocean-going ship alongside a coal pier is an intimidating modeling project, but there are ways to manage the scope of the project. The ships could be assumed to occupy a berth in the aisle, or they could be little more than flats or photo murals on a backdrop.

That leaves the piers and steel towers—admittedly lengthy but no more so than the ore unloading docks so often modeled by those who admire the Lake Superior & Ishpeming or the Duluth, Missabe & Iron Range, among other such ore haulers. Hoppers are shoved up a ramp by between-the-rail car pushers, rotated and dumped, then allowed to exit via a roller-coaster switchback track to an empties yard.

I've seen such facilities modeled, including some that actually dump the cars, which resolves the loads-in/ empties-out concern. If the main thrust of your railroad is the harbor area with its constant inbound movements of loaded hoppers and outbound movements of empties, spending extra time on a "centerpiece" LDE such as a coal unloading pier would be justified.

Pacific ports

The West Coast has several ports that offer outstanding LDE candidates. Keith Jordan documented the rail and marine operations around San Diego in the years just prior to World War II in a track plan that contains a number of LDEs, including the Santa Fe's mission-style depot and nearby Broadway Pier (fig. 9-12, page 86).

Byron Henderson explained the Alameda Belt Line's operations on an island in San Francisco Bay in *Model Railroad Planning 2005* and provided an LDE-based track plan (fig. 9-13, page 87). There were several other car ferry operations in the Bay Area that could also serve as equally promising LDE candidates.

Another James River line

The Surry, Sussex & Southampton was a colorful three-footer that hauled logs to what was once the largest hardwood saw mill on the East Coast at Dendron, Va. It also escorted peanuts to market and passengers to and from a connection with river boats at Scotland, just across from historic Jamestown (fig. 9-14).

The SS&S boasted several unique, or at least highly unusual, traits, including ganging up two or three 0-4-2 T tank engines instead of Shays or Heislers to haul the logs out of the woods. According to H. Temple Crittenden, who wrote a colorful history of the SS&S titled *The Comp'ny* (McClain Printing 1967), the railroad also employed a switchback in what was otherwise rather flat territory to get down to the pier that jutted out into the James River.

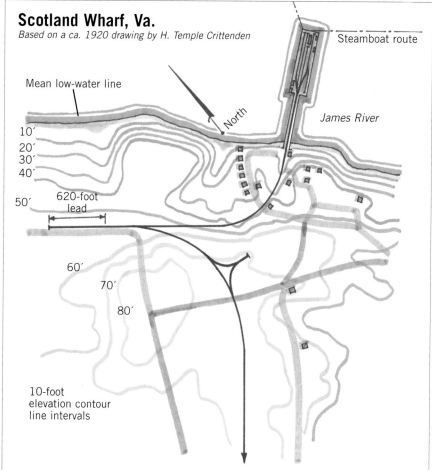

Scotland Wharf, Va.
Based on a ca. 1920 drawing by H. Temple Crittenden

Steamboat route

Mean low-water line

North

James River

10'
20'
30'
40'
50'

620-foot lead

60'
70'
80'

10-foot elevation contour line intervals

One of the most intriguing common carriers most modelers have never heard of was Virginia's Surry, Sussex & Southampton, which hauled timber and peanuts. Its east end was on a pier that jutted out into the James River at Scotland Wharf and was reached via a switchback down the river bank. Several of the railroad's steam locomotives have been preserved.

9-14

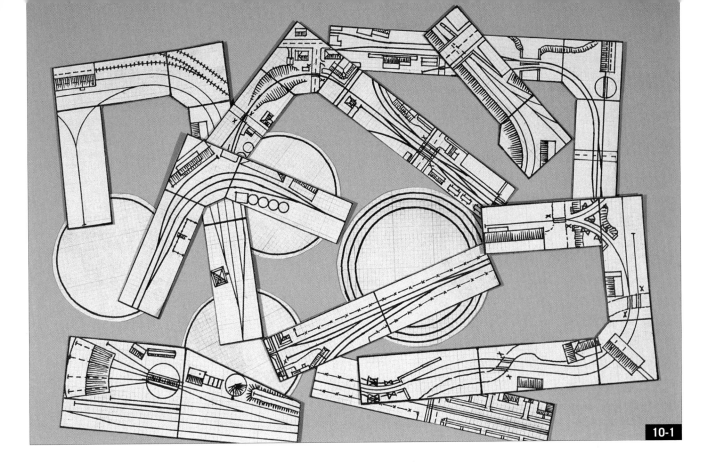

10-1

CHAPTER TEN

Using "puzzle pieces" to plan a layout

We've reviewed the concept behind Layout Design Elements, and we've explored various types of LDE candidates. Now, it's time to put what we've learned into practice by designing a layout. Actually, we'll look at not one but two model railroads that I designed by moving the LDE "puzzle pieces" shown in fig. 10-1 around on a floor plan of a typical bedroom. We can kill two birds (planning and construction) with one stone by using David Barrow's standard 18" x 48" dominoes (fig. 10-2) for many of the LDEs. His writings about dominoes in *Model Railroader* and *Model Railroad Planning* explain how they can be constructed and how to use them in almost any situation. Dominoes are almost certain to save a modeler a lot of time and head-scratching.

▲ The author used these Layout Design Element "puzzle pieces" of 48"-long "domino" components to create track plans for two bedroom-size railroads: a granger branch line in HO and a narrow-gauge Appalachian coal hauler in O scale.

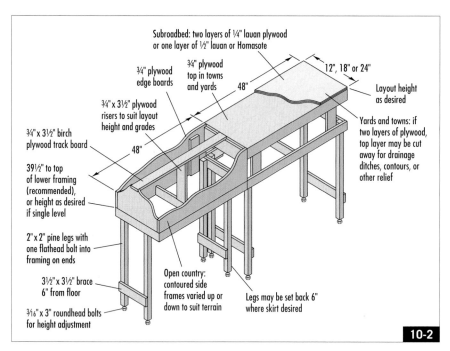

Subroadbed: two layers of ¼" lauan plywood
or one layer of ½" lauan or Homasote

¾" plywood
top in towns
and yards

¾" plywood
edge boards

12", 18" or 24"

48"

¾" x 3½" plywood
risers to suit layout
height and grades

Layout height
as desired

¾" x 3½"
birch plywood track board

48"

Yards and towns: if
two layers of plywood,
top layer may be cut
away for drainage
ditches, contours, or
other relief

39½" to top
of lower framing
(recommended),
or height as desired
if single level

2" x 2" pine legs with
one flathead bolt into
framing on ends

Open country:
contoured side
frames varied up or
down to suit terrain

3½" x 3½" brace
6" from floor

Legs may be set back 6"
where skirt desired

³⁄₁₆" x 3" roundhead bolts
for height adjustment

10-2

▲ David Barrow advocates building layouts of any size using four-foot-long "dominoes" of 12", 18", or 24" widths. The author used intermediate-width dominoes as the basis for the LDEs employed in the design of the HO Western Indiana Ry. and the On2½ Appalachian & Western.

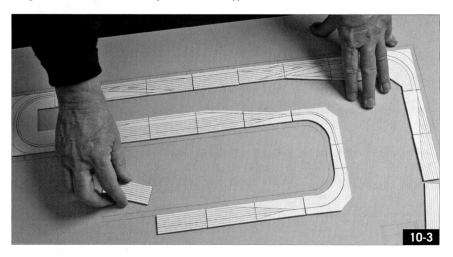

10-3

▲ David Barrow used puzzle pieces to explain his strategy behind domino-based layout design. The same approach applies to LDE-based layout design when the dominoes are patterned after actual prototype locations. Tommy Holt photo.

Theme and era

The first step in designing a track plan is to pick a theme for the railroad. For this exercise, I chose a freelanced granger branch line for an HO scale plan and a freelanced Appalachian short line for an On2½ (O scale, 2½-foot gauge) plan. It's somewhat easier to choose LDEs for a prototype-based layout, hence the focus here on freelanced railroads. Since I used LDEs based on prototypes from across the continent, the HO layout could represent any flatlands region, and the On2½ railroad could be located in any hilly or mountainous region.

To refine one's objectives, I recommend locating a freelanced railroad on an actual map of a region of the North American rail network. That makes it easier to find "gaps" where a new railroad might fit into the big picture, and you'll have a better understanding on how the railroad should look and what it does for a living. Knowing where the railroad lies in relation to its major connections and markets is a major plus.

Although both railroads are freelanced, it would be easy to convert either plan to follow a specific prototype. The HO plan, for example, uses two LDEs from the Nickel Plate's St. Louis Division, and the other LDEs could be exchanged for NKP-based sites. Similarly, the narrow-gauge layout could be converted to a prototype plan based on, say, the East Broad Top by swapping Robertsdale for Ridgway and using other EBT LDEs along the way. Or designing a layout starting with the Waynesburg Yard LDE for the Pennsylvania Railroad's Waynesburg

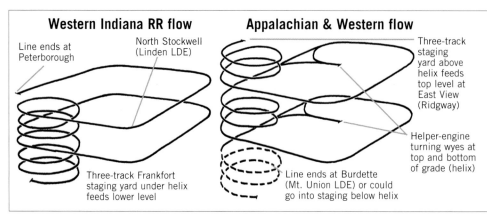

Western Indiana RR flow

Line ends at
Peterborough

North Stockwell
(Linden LDE)

Three-track Frankfort
staging yard under helix
feeds lower level

Appalachian & Western flow

Three-track
staging
yard above
helix feeds
top level at
East View
(Ridgway)

Helper-engine
turning wyes at
top and bottom
of grade (helix)

Line ends at Burdette
(Mt. Union LDE) or could
go into staging below helix

These schematic drawings show the "flow" of the trackwork in the HO and On2½ plans discussed in this chapter. Trains continue in the same direction around the room as they approach and leave the helix, thus maintaining their geographical direction; east is always to the right. Three-track staging yards are tucked under (WIRR) or over (A&W) the between-deck helix. **10-4**

& Washington line in southwestern Pennsylvania would be a natural using Bachmann's On2½ PRR equipment.

Selecting an era is the next step. The tight curves (I chose a 24" minimum for both layouts) favor short locomotives and cars, which leans toward but does not mandate the 1960s or earlier for the HO plan. The O scale narrow-gauge plan was designed around Bachmann's 2-6-0, so any period in the first half of the 20th century is fine. A larger locomotive such as Broadway Ltd.'s handsome D&RGW C-16 2-8-0 is more comfortable on 30" curves, which would require adjustments to the plan.

LDE candidates

Now comes the fun part: choosing candidates for Layout Design Elements. The unbridled freelancer can have a field day here, as there are no limits as to what could go where. Those who want their model railroads to accurately depict a specific region, era, and type of railroading, as is the case with prototype modeling and prototype-based freelancing, will need to be more selective.

Ideally, you should prepare scale drawings of more LDEs than you expect to have space for, as this will give you more flexibility. Moreover, you'll understand from the outset that everything won't fit, so there shouldn't be any self-generated pressure to cram every LDE into the space.

Drawing puzzle pieces

When a reasonable number of LDE candidates have been selected, they need to be converted to "puzzle pieces" that you can move around on a "game board"—a floor-plan drawing of the area in which you plan to fit your layout made to the same scale as the puzzle pieces (fig. 10-3).

I picked ¾" to the foot (each ¹⁄₁₆" equals one actual inch), which is large enough to work with yet small enough to fit most LDEs on standard-size graph paper. Having precise prototype dimensions of the LDE candidates is usually not critical at this stage, since a degree of selective compression is almost always required.

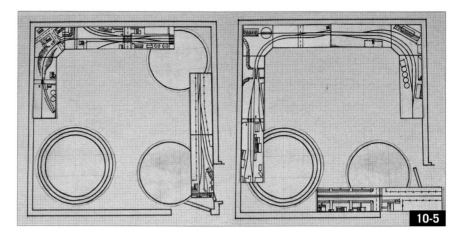

▲ Here are the LDEs for both levels of the HO Western Indiana RR in their final positions, which made it much easier to draw the track plan shown in fig. 10-7. Moving clockwise from lower left on the lower level (left photo), the LDEs are Linden, Cayuga, Elwood, Cottonwood, and Peterborough. The author accommodated the room's restricted dimensions by drawing L-shaped LDEs that combine 24"-square corner pieces with standard 18" x 48" dominoes. For longer walls, drawing strictly linear dominoes would have been easier and entirely adequate for planning purposes. Note, too, that both the Cayuga and Cottonwood LDEs have curves replicating those found on their prototypes, so their L-shape is appropriate.

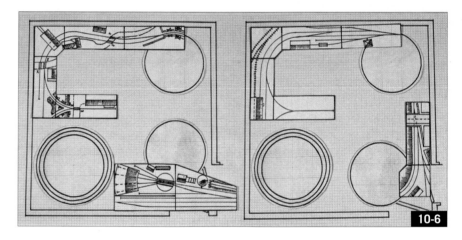

▲ The dominos for both levels of the On2½ Appalachian & Western were tailored to accommodate the relatively short walls with L-shaped LDEs. Clockwise from the lower-left corner of the upper level (left), the LDEs are Ridgway, Ophir, Spruce Pine, and Mt. Union. The Ridgway engine-terminal LDE is compact but still could not be fitted into the available space without curving it around one corner. The coal-cleaning plant at Mt. Union will highlight the huge size difference between standard- and narrow-car hoppers.

I made neat drawings of each LDE on graph paper. Doing this freehand, using the grid lines to ensure proper track spacing and reasonably straight lines, is fine. I used a triangle, compass, circle template, and French curve to help keep the lines neat, but that was mainly to ensure that they looked presentable in print.

I took care not to cheat on turnout angles; a no. 6 turnout, which I used for both plans, must be drawn by counting out six spaces, then going up one space. Fudging the turnout angle is

perhaps the most common error made when drawing a track plan. It's a good idea to select a brand of commercial track components, then measure the turnout's actual frog angle to ensure that your drawing will be accurate.

If you have computer-aided drafting (CAD) software for your personal computer, you can create the room shape and each LDE as an element, much like drawing a custom turnout, and move the LDEs around until you find a reasonable way to fit them together. The software prevents

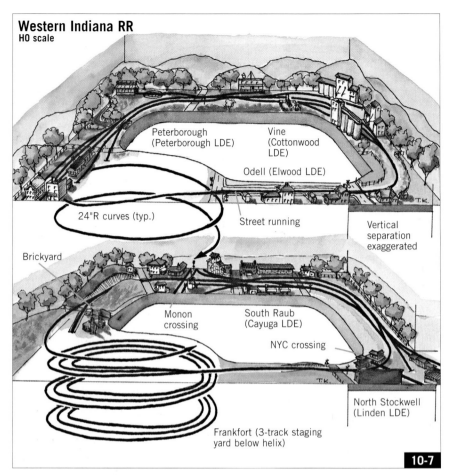

Western Indiana RR
HO scale

Peterborough
(Peterborough LDE)

Vine
(Cottonwood
LDE)

Odell (Elwood LDE)

24"R curves (typ.)

Street running

Vertical
separation
exaggerated

Brickyard

Monon
crossing

South Raub
(Cayuga LDE)

NYC crossing

North Stockwell
(Linden LDE)

Frankfort (3-track staging
yard below helix)

10-7

▲ The HO scale Western Indiana RR is a short line that heads west from the busy transportation hub at Frankfort, Ind. (helix staging below the lower level), and continues to the end of the line at Peterborough. Along the way it passes through "Linden," "Cayuga," "Cottonwood," and "Elwood" LDEs. Despite the coast-to-coast location of the LDE candidates, the author was able to embrace a Midwestern granger theme while retaining the basic prototypical track and structure arrangements. The low mountains on the upper-level backdrop show how easily the railroad could be set in a different region.

cheating with turnout angles, curve-tangent alignments, and so on.

I also drew several circles representing my minimum-radius curves (24" for both layouts) so I wouldn't have an excuse to cheat there, either. In the small room used for this exercise, there was little doubt that the curves would have to be tucked into the four corners. The main task was to fit various LDE candidates between or in those corners.

You'll note that there are no large classification yards on either plan. There simply wasn't space for both a reasonable mainline run between several towns and a large yard. But a yard may be so important to your style of operation that it deserves all the space it requires. In fact, a track plan that is simply a classification-yard

LDE fed at one or both ends by a staging yard may be a better match for your objectives.

Don't overlook the fact that passing, classification, and staging yard track lengths are all related. There's no sense designing a classification or staging yard to accommodate a 20-car train if your longest Town LDE has a 10-car passing track.

The spiral helix
The minimum-radius LDEs can also be used to represent a single-track spiral helix that climbs or descends between levels. A helix is a controversial bit of trackwork, however, as it requires care during construction and consumes a lot of trackwork—it often represents a significant proportion of the total mainline run.

A helix used at the open end of a peninsula may reverse the direction of a train running through a scene. If east is to the right (which suggests the sun is to your back, as it is in the northern hemisphere) as a train approaches a helix on the lower deck, it may emerge on the upper deck moving to the left—but still eastbound.

This can be an advantage if you're depicting a prototype location where the railroad shifts from one wall of a valley to the other at the same time the highway from which you view the railroad also swaps sides of the canyon. If the spiral is inserted near the point where the prototype line bridges the canyon (fig. 8-8) just as the model railroad goes between decks, one's point of view will automatically change from looking north to looking south.

To get around the fact that trains tend to disappear for considerable lengths of time as they climb or descend through a helix, one or two lobes of the helix can be extended out into a mini-scene. This allows crews to check that their trains are still moving at a reasonable pace.

I located the between-decks helix for both plans in one corner of the room at the midpoint of the run. After exiting the helix, the main line continues in the same direction around the room, which caused no undesired change of direction. Small windows could be cut into the fascia that screens the helix from view to allow crews to check on the progress of their trains.

I made no effort to connect the two ends of the railroad, but the presence of a helix makes this feasible for those who enjoy letting a train run continuously to entertain guests.

Helix staging
I didn't create separate staging yard LDEs for either plan, as I wanted to take advantage of the fact that the considerable amount of track inherent in a helix can be used for staging. Since I had already "used up" the floor space under the single-track helix needed to climb between levels, locating a three-track staging yard helix above the upper deck or below the lower deck wouldn't further encroach on the room.

Fig. 10-4 (page 90) shows how each railroad's main line flows from a staging helix, around the room, through a single-track helix to the other level, and then around the room.

Using puzzle pieces

I drew two sets of puzzle pieces, one for the HO layout, the other for the On2½ layout, on graph paper to the same scale as a floor plan of the layout room. Figs. 10-5 and 10-6 (page 91) show how I arranged them to help me design the final track plans.

Several of the LDEs fit on a pair of David Barrow's standard 18" x 48" dominoes. Since I knew that I couldn't fit the longer LDEs such as Cayuga and Mt. Union along any single wall of the room, I drew them to include a 24"-square corner piece plus a third domino at right angles to the first.

It's important to understand that, in so doing, I essentially skipped an intermediate step whereby I would have tried to fit a lengthy LDE into the room, found it too long, and then mentally "bent" it around a corner. Had the room been larger, I would not have taken time to do such LDE customization at this early stage of layout planning.

Even some shorter LDEs such as the Ridgway roundhouse dominoes proved too long for the remaining space next to the helix or closet door, however. In such cases, I simply located the LDEs in the corner with the understanding that I'd have to bend them to fit around a curve when I drew up the final track plans.

All LDEs were photocopied and then mounted on cardstock for durability using 3M spray glue. I cut them out and sorted them into two piles, one for each railroad. Using two copies of the floor plan, one for each level, I moved each set of LDEs around to see what could fit where.

The result was a pair of freelanced railroads: "The Western Indiana RR" and "The Appalachian & Western Ry." Both use LDE candidates previously described in this book, and the accompanying descriptions offer insights to the design parameters.

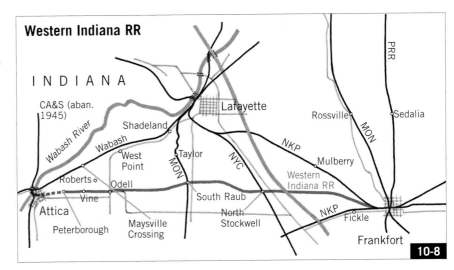

▲ Literally putting a freelanced railroad on the map ensures that its connections and major routes to customers can be identified. This map of western Indiana shows that the freelanced Western Indiana RR heads west out of Frankfort between two NKP divisions and crosses the NYC and Monon before reaching Peterborough just east of Attica. Perhaps the line once continued into Attica to connect with the Wabash and the Chicago, Attica & Southern before the latter was abandoned in 1945.

Changing scales

Note that either one of the two track plans I created using LDEs could be built in N scale simply by reducing the track centerline spacing. A bonus is that every track would effectively double in length, allowing the use of longer trains, or you could shorten the tracks to create open areas.

Similarly, the On2½ plan could be converted to HO standard gauge by reducing the track spacing from 3" to 2". In both cases, the curves would automatically seem much broader. Going the other way by changing the HO plan to On2½ would require spacing the tracks another inch apart and ensuring that the considerably larger structures would fit.

Design a new railroad

Most of us learn more by actually doing rather than by merely observing. I therefore recommend that, after reviewing the track plans I created as examples of the layout-design process using LDEs, you use the same LDEs plus a few more of your own choosing to create new track plans.

You may decide to fit them into the spare room's footprint I used, but you might learn more by making a scale drawing of a new room plan that matches the space you've been eyeing for your next layout. Make two or more

copies of the floor plan if you plan to design a multi-level layout.

If the room is large enough, you can have the main line climb continuously in one direction from one end of the railroad to the other, as is the case with my NKP track plan (which appeared in the September and October 2000 issues of Model Railroader). This technique usually works well only when you have a long mainline run. To climb, say, a bare minimum of 12" between decks on a 2-percent grade (2" of climb for every 100" of run) requires a run of 600", or 50 feet. Double that to 4 percent, which is a very stiff grade, and you still need a run of 25 feet. For smaller rooms, you'll therefore need to use a helix to climb between decks on a reasonable grade.

What's "reasonable"? Consider this: An engine that will claw its way up a steep grade may "buck" like crazy coming back down it as the "play" in the gear train runs in and out. This is especially true if there's a heavy train pushing the engine down the hill. Although thrust washers in the gearbox may help to alleviate such problems, it pays to build a test track that includes typical grades and curves to see how the locomotives you plan to use actually perform up and down the hill with typical trains in tow.

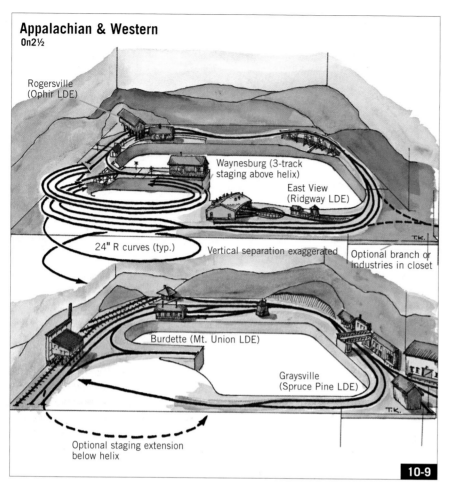

Appalachian & Western
On2½

Rogersville
(Ophir LDE)

Waynesburg (3-track
staging above helix)

East View
(Ridgway LDE)

24" R curves (typ.) Vertical separation exaggerated

Optional branch or
industries in closet

T.K.

Burdette (Mt. Union LDE)

Graysville
(Spruce Pine LDE)

T.K.

Optional staging extension
below helix

10-9

▲ This On2½ plan for the freelanced Appalachian & Western was designed by arranging a series of mountain-based LDEs on two levels connected by a helix. The railroad begins in a three-track helix staging yard on the upper level representing Waynesburg, Pa., heads west to its outlying engine terminal in "Ridgway" (East View) where a truncated branch or industrial spurs could head into the closet. It then continues under a mine tipple at "Ophir" (Rogersville), where there's a wye to turn helpers preparing to head back down the mountain. After descending the helix, the line runs through "Spruce Pine" (Graysville) with its industrial spurs extending into the closet, and then terminates at "Mt. Union" (Burdette) with its coal-cleaning plant, engine-turning wye, and freelanced standard-gauge connection. The line ends in stub-ended staging tracks under the bottom turn of the helix, but it could be extended into a larger staging yard built as yet another helix under the main helix (see fig. 10-4).

The Western Indiana RR

Let's review the steps I used to convert the HO LDEs shown in fig. 10-5 into the track plan shown in fig. 10-7 (page 92).

To get oriented, I needed to draw the WIRR on a map of western Indiana (fig. 10-8, page 93). As a guide, I used the *Indiana Atlas & Gazetteer*, a detailed map book published by DeLorme (www.delorme.com), which shows highways, railroads (including some abandoned lines), water courses, and contour lines. I went to college at Purdue and was therefore familiar with the area, and I knew that no railroad

extended straight west out of Frankfort, Ind., which the atlas confirmed.

I assumed the WIRR was a shortline railroad serving several towns with grain elevators and a few other industries typical of the Midwest. I set its eastern terminus in Frankfort, a transportation hub where two divisions of the Nickel Plate Road crossed each other as well as the Monon and Pennsylvania. This ensured plenty of interchange traffic.

I then ran the WIRR west out of Frankfort and had it peter out at "Peterborough," where—like its prototype—it has a turntable to turn

steam power. Mythical Peterborough, Ind., was located just east of Attica; like the B&M through the real Peterborough, N. H., perhaps the line used to continue—in this case, west a few miles to Attica to connect with the Wabash and another short line, the Chicago, Attica & Southern. Along the way, the Western Indiana serves several communities selected from LDE candidates we've previously discussed.

With the railroad on a map, I needed to make a list of suitable LDE candidates. It would have been fun to take a field trip to visit actual communities in the part of the Midwest being considered, and then to design LDEs based on them. That might have caused me to revise the route to accommodate outstanding candidates not originally considered. I would probably have renamed some of the towns and, as Bill Darnaby did at Edison, Ohio (fig. 7-7), retain the name and prototype trackage in others while superimposing the WIRR.

For this exercise, however, I wanted to use examples from the previous chapters, and I ignored those with a mountainous or port theme. Among those that looked promising were Linden, Ind. (NKP-Monon interchange), Cayuga, Ind. (water tower, NKP-C&EI interchange, and several industries), Elwood, Ind. (main line down the center of a street), Cottonwood, Idaho (grain elevators in a "corner"), and Peterborough, N. H. (small terminal with several industries at the end of a branch).

Where practical, I used the 18" x 48" dimensions of the standard Barrow domino or a 24"-square corner section. The room is just under 12 feet in both dimensions, so at least one section had to be made an inch or two shorter.

The railroad starts in a three-track staging yard representing Frankfort constructed as a helix below the lower level. It emerges at the west end of the railroad's main classification yard at WY Tower, which is where the NKP's mains to Peoria and St. Louis split apart.

On the removable benchwork section in front of the entry door and closet is "North Stockwell" (fig. 2-2), which is the Linden, Ind., LDE. Here the WIRR crosses the New York Central's Indianapolis line. To increase the capacity of the interchange, I extended the tracks into the closet.

Around the bend from Linden is "South Raub," an LDE based on Cayuga, Ind. (fig. 2-7), where there's an interchange with a crossing double-track railroad. The foreign road could be single-tracked to represent the Monon, as the WIRR map suggests. There's also a lumberyard, Standard Oil unloading facility (fig. 4-16), a grain elevator, and a brickyard (fig. 4-17). By connecting the North Stockwell and South Raub passing tracks, longer trains can be accommodated.

Equally important, "Cayuga" (South Raub) has a water tank where steam locomotives can refill their tenders before tackling the hill (helix to the top level) west of town. The NKP's curving westbound climb out of the Wabash River valley at Cayuga is why I picked that LDE candidate for this location. In the days when this part of the railroad was operated with 2-8-0s, a helper engine was stationed at Cayuga, and we could emulate that practice here.

Let's do some math to be sure there is sufficient clearance between turns in the helix. The circumference of the 24"-radius circle can be calculated by multiplying the diameter (48") by pi (3.14), which is about 150". If the grade is set at 2 percent, then .02 x 150" = 3" of height is gained for every complete circle of the helix. That's adequate clearance, but just barely, when the thickness of the subroadbed is subtracted.

The grade could probably be increased to 2.5 percent without requiring the use of helpers, which might seem odd on a granger branch line. Testing the actual steam locomotives you plan to use on a mock-up of this curving grade would be mandatory before setting the gradient to preclude rude surprises. (In the diesel era, of course, another unit could be added to the consist without raising eyebrows.)

Westbounds emerge from the helix into an LDE featuring trackage down the middle of a street through "Odell," based on Elwood, Ind. (fig. 7-21),

cross in front of the entry door, and enter "Vine," which is based on the Cottonwood, Ida., LDE (fig. 2-13). The prototypical curve through town makes it an ideal LDE candidate for use in a corner of a room.

To ensure adequate length, I extended the Vine passing track west into "Peterborough" (fig. 2-15), which is the end of the branch (as was its prototype after the line north of town was severed by a flood). A turntable allows steam locomotives to be reversed for the trip back to Frankfort.

Note that I used LDE candidates scattered across the U.S. from New Hampshire through Indiana to Idaho without creating any visual or operational oddities. And I avoided having to invent trackage arrangements, as the prototype proved to be an excellent guide. Done with care, "mixing and matching" LDEs is thus a practical way to increase the options available to the designer of a freelanced railroad.

To underscore the versatility, I sketched low mountains on the backdrop of the upper level, as would be appropriate if the layout were located in New England (like Peterborough) or the Northwest (like Cottonwood). Adding similar mountains to the lower level's backdrop would effectively transport it to another locale.

The Appalachian & Western Ry.

Now let's use LDE candidates that are more reflective of mountain railroading for the On2½ Appalachian & Western Ry. (fig. 10-9). Since crossings with foreign roads are infrequent, we'll look for other operational challenges such as helper grades.

After poring over DeLorme's Pennsylvania atlas and reviewing the LDE candidates presented in this book, I located the mythical line in the southwest corner of the Commonwealth (fig. 10-10). The A&W is assumed to have served as a northwesterly extension of the narrow-gauge Waynesburg & Washington. Perhaps the A&W, like the Waynesburg & Washington and the Ohio River & Western, has been

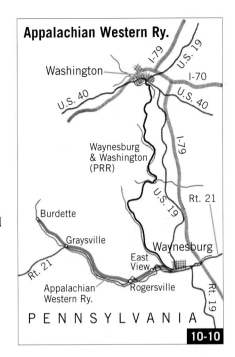

▲ The freelanced Appalachian & Western heads northwest out of Waynesburg, Pa., along South Fork and Grays Fork through the actual towns of East View, Rogersville, and Graysville to Burdette. Field trips to the area might uncover modeling opportunities that complement the LDEs; this part of Pennsylvania boasts a number of covered road bridges, for example.

absorbed by the mighty Pennsylvania.

Why On2½? Many modelers, especially those of bifocal age, appreciate the large size of O scale models but don't feel they have enough space for a 1:48 standard-gauge layout. On2½ models are designed to run on HO gauge track, however, and most of the commercial offerings to date will negotiate relatively tight HO curves such as the 24" radius I used here. Bachmann's extensive On2½ line is or has been offered factory painted for the Pensylvania RR.

For those wanting something a little off the beaten path, kitbashing HO diesels and steam (especially geared "logging" locomotives such as Shays and Heislers)—often simply by adding a larger cab—is a popular approach to fleshing out an On2½ roster (fig. 10-11, page 96). Such locomotives will negotiate extremely sharp curves, not to mention climb steep grades, which makes it possible to operate O scale models in a space previously considered adequate only for a much smaller scale.

Steve Sherrill kitbashed HO locomotives for use on his On2½ Shady Grove & Sherrill by making new shells or by adding larger cabs, stacks, and domes, as on Heisler 6. Such engines will negotiate tight curves and climb steep grades. Bill Miller photos **10-11**

Track centerlines do need to be spaced a bit farther apart, however. Bill Miller, who with his wife, Mary, operates both On3 and On2½ railroads on one layout, recommends using 3" between centerlines, as opposed to 2" in HO scale.

Slim-gauge railroads that eked out a living in the mountains tended to have a lot in common, including an obvious lack of prosperity in their later years. To underscore this cross-country commonality, two of the LDE candidates—Ridgway and Ophir on the Rio Grande Southern (figs. 6-1 and 7-19)—hail from the West. Their names are too well known to be retained on an Eastern railroad.

At the upper end of the railroad where the A&W connects to another (staged) carrier, emulating the D&RGW-to-RGS connection at Ridgway, I didn't have room for a yard, so I picked an engine-terminal LDE instead and called it East View for a town west of Waynesburg, Pa. (fig. 5-1).

On the opposite wall from

10-12

▲ The author built the HO Coal Fork Extension of the Allegheny Midland on 16"- to 24"-wide benchwork above bookcases, which was deep enough to model typical heavily forested Appalachian ridges.

East View/Ridgway is the town of Rogersville, an actual town that, ahem, miraculously resembles Ophir, Colo. (fig. 7-19). I chose Ophir as an LDE candidate because, like Cottonwood, it fits nicely into a corner of the room. Moreover, its over-the-track mining structure could stand in for an Appalachian coal tipple. In this case, the load-out siding is across the main line from the depot.

Helpers need to be turned at the bottom and top of the helper grade up the helix. Before even trying to move the puzzle-pieces around on the game board, I combined the L-shaped Ophir corner LDE with a wye to confirm they would fit in the available space. The wye dominoes could fold down or "plug in" to free up the center of the room for everyday use as a bedroom or home office.

As the railroad exits the bottom end of the single-track helix, it enters Graysville, again gleaned from a Pennsylvania topo map—actually the Spruce Pine LDE (fig. 2-23). I narrowed the gauge a bit through this Clinchfield town and located it so that its several industrial spurs could extend back into the closet.

On the downhill end of the Appalachian & Western at Burdette, Pa., is an LDE based on the East Broad Top–Pennsylvania interchange and coal cleaning plant at Mt. Union, Pa. (fig. 5-16). Only one standard- and one narrow-gauge track will fit under the truncated preparation plant, but you can spot a string of standard-gauge hoppers alongside the slim-gauge cars to call attention to the considerable difference in size.

Note that the main line starts to climb near the room entrance door to the right of the helix. This allows the first turn of the helix to gain enough elevation to clear the EBT–PRR staging below it. This points out another planning difference between HO and On2½: vertical clearances.

Bill Miller measured an On3 C-16 and recommends a minimum of 3¾" clearance—"and 4" would be better," he added. I retained the 24" minimum radius of the HO plan, so the circumference stays the same at 150". To create a 4" separation between each turn of the helix requires a grade of 4" divided by 150", or 3 percent as a bare minimum when the subroadbed's thickness is added.

This grade will probably require a second 2-6-0 used as a pusher, which is a bonus: Adding helpers at the bottom of the hill and removing them at the summit effectively lengthens each run.

One last point: The 18" width of the dominoes might seem restricting for mountainous scenery, but I built the Coal Fork Extension of the Allegheny Midland on shelves that were only 16" to 24" wide (fig. 10-12).

Portable tool kit

Now that you've mastered the basics of the Layout Design Element approach to layout design, it's time to enjoy using these new additions to your planning tool box. I hope that you find the LDE approach to track planning to be a useful and even entertaining tool. Perhaps you'll share your experiences and track plans with the rest of us through the pages of *Model Railroader* or *Model Railroad Planning*.